KAIROS

KAIROS

Three Prophetic Challenges to the Church

edited by

Robert McAfee Brown

WILLIAM B. EERDMANS PUBLISHING COMPANY
GRAND RAPIDS, MICHIGAN

Reprinted, November 1992

The Kairos Document: Challenge to the Church (Revised Second Edition)
first published 1986 by Skotaville Publishers, Braamfontein, and Wm. B.
Eerdmans Publishing Co., Grand Rapids, Mich., and published jointly 1987
by Wm. B. Eerdmans Publishing Company and Theology in Global Context
Association, New York.

Kairos Central America: A Challenge to the Churches of the World first
published 1988 by New York Circus Publications, Inc.

The Road to Damascus: Kairos and Conversion first published July 1989 by
Catholic Institute for International Relations (CIIR), London; Center of Con-
cern, Washington, D.C.; and Christian Aid, London. International © Catholic
Institute for International Relations 1989; US © Center of Concern 1989.

Printed in the United States of America

Contents

v

Acknowledgments

Thanks are extended to the New York Circus, Inc., for permission to publish *Kairos Central America,* and to the Center of Concern for permission to publish *The Road to Damascus.* Any royalties from the present volume will go through them to groups that originated the two documents, and to the Institute for Contextual Theology in South Africa, which coordinated the writing of the initial *Kairos Document.*

The Committee of Correspondence, growing out of the Kirkridge Conference mentioned in the "Conclusion," and the Community of St. Martin have provided unpublished materials of particular help to the editor. Special thanks are extended to Jack Nelson-Pallmeyer for overseeing attempts to coordinate work on a *Kairos USA* document, and for invaluable help in the creation of the present volume.

Those of us in the United States need to remain permanently humbled and challenged by the courage of the original signers of these documents, who in many instances were risking their lives by public association with their content. We can only pray that some of their courage will rub off on us.

The Editor

The Recovery of *Kairos*

1. From the Periphery to the Center

In the great missionary expansion of the nineteenth century, Christians from North America and Europe went to Asia, Africa, and Latin America to take the good news of salvation. Claiming that they were at the "center" of Christian civilization, they went out to the "periphery," the edge, as far as necessary so that no one would be excluded from their outreach.

The imagery dominated the church's understanding of itself for a long time. After World War II, for example, when the World Council of Churches came into being, the three official languages for World Council meetings were English, French, and German, those languages most spoken at the center, and members from the periphery had to adapt themselves linguistically to one of those languages if they expected a serious hearing.

But what has happened (and the World Council of Churches has itself been a splendid exemplar of the shift) is that the creative thrust of the gospel has begun to move in precisely the opposite direction. The centers of new vitality in the church are now at what is still (rather patronizingly) called the periphery, while those most in need of the infusions of vitality are those dwelling at what is still (even more patronizingly) called the center. The earlier recipients of the gospel are the new givers of the gospel, while the earlier givers are the new recipients.

Much the same thing has happened in theology. For generations (or so it seemed) new theological insights were born in Germany, gradually made their way to Britain and thence to the United States, perhaps or perhaps not to gain a foothold in what was later called the "Third World" beyond the shores of Europe and North America. But today, if one asks, "Where are the new theological currents originating?" the answer comes readily: "In the Third World, in Latin America, Asia, and Africa, usually in a variant of liberation theology." A straw in the wind: in theological education in the United States, the long, undisputed reign of German as "*the* theological language" is being challenged by Spanish.

Without claiming that the *kairos* documents contained herein are exclusively examples of liberation theology (though the claim could be floated and perhaps sustained), it can be claimed that they represent yet another instance of the reality that those on the periphery (i.e. South Africa, Central America, and Asia) are speaking powerful words that those in the center (i.e., the rest of us) have no choice but to take seriously.

Since the original *Kairos Document: Challenge to the Church* was issued in South Africa in 1985, two similar documents have appeared: *Kairos Central America* in 1988, and *The Road to Damascus: Kairos and Conversion* (a product of South African, Central American, and Asian cocreation) in 1989. Another *kairos* document is being developed in Europe, and yet another in the Middle East. There may be still more on the way. And sooner or later a *kairos* document from the United States must be forthcoming, to respond to what Christians in other parts of the world have been writing to us and about us. One of the not-so-hidden agenda items of the present volume is to enlist support for such a venture.

2. What Is a *Kairos*?

The theological word *kairos* (like so many other theological words) is simply the transliteration of a Greek word for "time," a very special kind of time. It is usually contrasted with another transliterated Greek word for time, *chronos,* from which we derive several familiar English words such as "chronology" and "chronological." *Chronos* stands for ordinary time, "clock-time," the succession of moments by means of which we divide our lives into seconds, minutes, hours, days, months, years, decades, centuries, eons. It is a tidy word; when we ask, "What time is it?" we can be assured of a clear-cut answer: "Twenty-one minutes past eleven," or "Just time for the six o'clock news," or "He ran the hundred yard dash in 9.6 seconds."

Kairos in the Bible

Things are not so tidy when we examine *kairos.* The word is used in the Bible to refer to a "right" time, a "special" time, when momentous things are happening or about to happen, in response to which we must make decisions that are likely to have far-reaching consequences. A *kairos,* then, is a time of opportunity demanding a response: God offers us a new set of possibilities and *we* have to accept or decline. John Marsh describes the use of the word in the New Testament: "The time of Jesus is *kairos*—and so it is a time of opportunity. To embrace the opportunity means salvation, to neglect it disaster. There is no third choice" (in Richardson, ed., *A Theological Word Book of the Bible,* p. 252).

Such an overview can be made more specific by looking at a few biblical examples.

The clearest one occurs near the beginning of Mark's Gospel, in the first recorded words of Jesus' public ministry: "The *kairos* is fulfilled, and the Kingdom of God is at hand. Repent and believe the gospel" (Mark 1:15). The promises of the past are coming to fulfillment in the present; something brand-new is breaking into human experience, and all who hear the announcement must do something about it. Jesus makes clear what the appropriate response is: repent, turn about, begin again, believe the good news.

The same emphasis is found in Paul's letters. He reminds those in Corinth that "Now is the acceptable *kairos;* behold, now is the day of salvation" (2 Cor. 6:2), and their response—and ours—as Paul writes elsewhere, must be to "redeem the *kairos*" (cf. Eph. 5:16; Col. 4:5), to seize the moment and respond appropriately.

But there is nothing automatic about it. One could initially discern the *kairos* and then backslide: Jesus contrasts the various kinds of soil onto which his message falls: "And the ones on the rock are those who, when they hear the word, receive it with joy, but these have no root, they believe for a while and in the *kairos* of temptation fall away" (Luke 8:13).

It is frequently suggested that the *kairos,* if not already here, is imminent, and that one must keep alert for its coming so as not to miss it: "Take heed, watch and pray, for you do not know when the *kairos* will come" (Luke 13:22). Paul echoes this theme: "I mean, brethren, the appointed *kairos* has grown very short" (1 Cor. 7:29), and this theme of the imminence of the *kairos* is found also at the beginning of the last book of the New Testament ("Blessed are those who read . . . hear and keep what is written therein, for the *kairos* is near"), and at the end as well ("And he said to me, 'Do not seal up the words of the prophecy of this book, for the *kairos* is near'") (Rev. 1:3 and 22:10 respectively).

So all who can discern the signs of the weather with skill must become equally adept at "discerning the signs of the *kairos*" (Matt. 16:3; cf. Luke 12:5).

But people do not necessarily discern correctly. The opportunity may be offered to them only to have them reject it. As Jesus is approaching Jerusalem he reflects on the consequences for those who miss the "appointed time," the *kairos:* "Your enemies will dash you to the ground, you and your children with you, and they will not leave one stone upon another in you. . . ." Why not? The verse continues in sober tones: ". . . because you did not know the *kairos* of your visitation" (Luke 19:44).

Kairos and Paul Tillich

It was in this mood of not wanting to miss the *kairos* that Paul Tillich, a young German military chaplain in World War I (who later became one of the most influential theologians of our time), reclaimed this uniquely biblical understanding of time, in the hope of understanding post–World War I Europe. He saw it as a time containing both theological and political possibilities, which converged for him in the hope for what he called "religious socialism." Tillich felt that Europe stood on the edge of a *kairos,* a time that God was seeking to use, and to which humanity was called upon to respond—an historical era in which a new *political* order responsive to religious concerns, and a new *religious* sensibility deeply immersed in the political order, could join forces. And the tragedy for Tillich—and, indeed, for all of Europe—was that the *kairos* did not come (or if it came, Europeans failed to recognize it). The moment passed, and instead of a break-through with a convergence between human and divine impulses, the consequences of the ensuing vacuum were Adolf Hitler, the death camps, World War II, and the era of the Cold War.

Kairos in the Documents

In our day Christians in many parts of the world have decided that we are in another *kairos,* another historical situation fraught with new possibilities. They want to make sure that this time the *kairos* does not pass by unattended, and they are seeking, through what they call "*kairos* documents," to alert the rest of us to the momentous nature of the times in which we live, and the necessity of responding appropriately.

Each document offers its own understanding of the word. Perhaps the clearest statement is in the Explanatory Notes to the South African document:

> *Kairos* is the Greek word that is used in the Bible to designate a special moment of time when God visits [God's] people to offer them a unique opportunity for repentance and conversion, for change and decisive action. It is a time of judgment. It is a moment of truth, a crisis. (Cf. p. 26 below.)

This is fleshed out in the main body of the text:

> For very many Christians in South Africa, this is the KAIROS, the moment of grace and opportunity, the favorable time in which God issues a challenge to decisive action. It is a danger-ous time because, if this opportunity is missed, and allowed to pass by, the loss for the Church, for the Gospel and for all the people of South Africa will be immeasurable. Jesus wept over Jerusalem. He wept over the tragedy of the destruction of the city and the massacre of the people that was imminent, "and

all because you did not recognize your opportunity *(kairos)* when God offered it." (Lk. 19:44)

The *Kairos Central America* document notes four converging opportunities:

Never before in our history have *the poor* felt themselves so moved by the Wind of the Spirit to be effective instruments for the purposes of the God who is Creator of all.

Never before have *the churches* of Central America felt themselves so engaged and challenged by the God of the poor.

Never before has *the Empire* [i.e., the First World and especially the United States] had to turn so irrationally to "might makes right."

Never before has *the world* had such a generalized feeling of international solidarity and shared responsibility in the face of what is in play in Central America, in the face of what this land is giving birth to for the sake of a New Humanity and a new world. (Para. 85, italics added)

Central American writers agree with their South African counterparts that the stakes are immeasurably high. It is an either/or situation:

Central America has become a Kairos of unforeseeable consequences: either we close the door on the possibility of hope for the poor for many years, or as prophets we open up a new Day for humanity and thus for the Church. (Para. 86)

Carefully chosen participial verbs describe an active God enlisting support for new and risky ventures. People are being called ". . . to discover the presence of God *walking* at the head of our people, *awakening* our desires to be free, *pushing* us along liberation paths, *defending* us from our oppressors, *supplying* us with what we need amid the desert's scarcity while we escape beyond [the] Empire's reach" (para. 93, italics added).

The *Road to Damascus* document particularly reminds us of the decisiveness of the moment:

> God is on the side of the poor, the oppressed, the persecuted.
> When this faith is proclaimed and lived in a situation of political
> conflict between the rich and the poor, and when the rich and
> the powerful reject this faith and condemn it as heresy, we can
> read the signs and discern something more than a crisis. We are
> faced with a *kairos*, a moment of truth, a time for decision, a
> time of grace, a God-given opportunity for conversion and hope.
> (Para. 43)

Saul, on the road to Damascus, faced his own personal *kairos*, which
was the need to choose between a God who sided with the religious
and political authorities who killed Jesus, and a God who sided with
One who was crucified as a blasphemer. That is precisely the *kairos*
our world faces:

> This *kairos* on the road to Damascus must be taken seriously
> by all who in the name of God support the persecution of
> Christians who side with the poor. The call to conversion is
> loud and clear. (Para. 86)

3. What Is a *Status Confessionis?*

Let us approach the sense of urgency in another way.

As 2,000 years of history demonstrate, Christians have a depress-
ing ability to occupy all sides of every controversial question. There
have been Christian defenses of war *and* pacifism, of fealty to kings
and to democratic experiments, of slavery *and* "abolition," of capitalism *and* socialism, of imperialism *and* trade agreements, of "pro-
life" *and* "pro-choice."

But every now and then the issues become so clear, and the stakes
so high, that the privilege of amiable disagreement must be super-
seded by clear-cut decisions, and the choice must move from
"both/and" to "either/or." Such a time is called a *status confessionis*,
a "confessional situation."

The most notable instance of a *status confessionis* in recent times
was the decision of the Confessing Church in Germany that it was
no longer possible to support Hitler and still claim the name of
Christian. Those who claimed the name of Christian had to be against

Hitler. The debate was over. The results were in. The verdict had been rendered.

This decision was embodied in a document issued in May 1934 that was called "The Barmen Declaration," consisting of six affirmations and six negations (see Appendix C for the text of the document). The Declaration was a very theological statement, written chiefly by Karl Barth, a Swiss theologian who at the time was teaching in Germany, and it forever disposes of the spurious claim that theology and politics can be separated, for it was highly political as well as theological. Its main thrust can be seen by examining the first affirmation and negation. The affirmation goes:

> Jesus Christ, as he is attested for us in Holy Scripture, is the one Word of God which we have to hear and which we have to trust and obey in life and death.

That sounds theological all right, but hardly political. However, when we read the accompanying negation, the political implications of the theological affirmation begin to take shape:

> We reject the false doctrine, as though the Church could and would have to acknowledge as a source of its proclamation, apart from and besides this one Word of God, still other events and powers, figures and truths, as God's revelation.

In the year and a half that he had been in power, Hitler had been able to claim everything the negation was refuting—i.e., trust *was* to be found for the Germans "apart from and besides this one Word of God," i.e., in the Nazi party itself; and it *was* "in other events, and powers, figures and truths," i.e., the Nazi ideology and its leaders, that the salvation of Germany was to be located. What this boiled down to for the signatories was that in saying Yes to Jesus Christ they were also saying No to Adolf Hitler. The leaders of the Nazi party saw very clearly what was at stake; many of the signatories were imprisoned, and some of them killed, as a result. The message of the church in that time of crisis, whatever the dangers, was not "both/and," but *either/or.*"

Another recent invoking of the *status confessionis* has been in the struggle over *apartheid* in South Africa. For generations, the South

African churches held that one could be a good Christian and support *apartheid,* and that someone else could be a good Christian and denounce *apartheid.* On the matter of *apartheid* and Christian faith the church's position was both/and.

But the longer the internal debate went on, the clearer it became to many within the church that such equivocation would not do. *Apartheid* was immoral, un-Christian, untrue, and immensely cruel. So, after much debate in a global organization to which many South African churches belonged, the World Alliance of Reformed Churches, that body formally declared in 1982 that *apartheid* was a heresy, an unacceptable distortion of Christian faith, which meant that it could no longer be claimed as a genuine article of Christian faith and belief, and that any who so claimed it excluded themselves by that action from membership in the church. To say Yes to Jesus Christ was to say No to *apartheid.* End of discussion.

So a *status confessionis* takes on the characteristics of a time of *kairos.* The two words point in similar directions: there come times when the situation is so grave, so fraught with radical consequences, that fence-sitting is no longer possible.

One must be for or against.

4. What Are the *Kairos* Documents?

All three *kairos* documents come out of situations of great turmoil, from which they attempt to speak a prophetic word to the church. Each comes from a different context, a different set of local circumstances, and therefore each has a different flavor. But the problems they deal with are distressingly similar—evil seems able to dwell in at least three places simultaneously. So, with whatever regional differences, the documents share certain things in common, and if we are aware of some of these we will be better able to approach them individually.

Shared Characteristics

1. All of the documents are written out of a sense of *urgency.* Matters of life and death are under discussion. Things are so bad that silence

is impossible and words (however far short they inevitably fall of communicating the full reality) must be uttered. Time is short. To fail to grasp the immediacy of the crisis means to be passed by and fail the test.

2. All of the documents are *the result of a group process,* involving consultations and discussions and drafting and redrafting by literally hundreds of persons. They have not emanated from a tiny elite corps offering a "theology for the masses." They are the masses doing theology for themselves. Nor are they "establishment" documents, commissioned by official church bodies and representing the seasoned convictions of the hierarchy. The signers come from a wide variety of faith convictions, ecclesiastical memberships, races, classes, colors, and degrees of learning.

3. All of the documents *begin by analyzing the present situation,* which in every case is one of oppression and pain. They do not start with lofty "theological analysis" or a reiteration of eternal (and abstract) truths. They are immersed in the immediacy and here-and-now character of what is going on in their own lives. Their descriptions vary, since the geographical and political contexts vary, but for all of them "the present situation" is a time of *kairos.*

4. All of the documents implicitly accept Gustavo Gutiérrez's claim that *theology is "the second act,"* preceded by active engagement with, and commitment to, the poor and oppressed. When the writers analyze the present situation, it is one in which they have lived and suffered themselves. When they come to theology—critical reflection on what they are doing in the light of the Word of God—it is solid, deep, and discernibly biblical and Christian theology. Time-honored Christian affirmations about God, human nature, sin, redemption, ecclesiology, and eschatology are related not in the abstract categories of Western establishment thought, but in the concrete, dynamic terms of their own situation, in which they feel that God is actively present and at work alongside of them. (Chapter Two of *The Road to Damascus,* "The Faith of the Poor," is a particularly vivid example of this trait.)

5. All of the documents *inform their theology by social analysis.* They seek to understand where God has placed them in the light of the social dynamics of violence, exploitation, justice, oppression, class struggle, community, martyrdom, signs of hope. A crucial point:

this does not mean that theology is reduced to social analysis, but that social analysis enriches theology, so that it is relevant to the specific situation. Sin, for example, is found not only in individual human hearts, but in social structures as well (in terms reminiscent of Paul's recognition of "the principalities and powers" that wreak such havoc in human life). An understanding of the *historical* development of structures of injustice, evil nations and empires, systems like apartheid and exploitive corporations, is crucial if Christians are to understand how social structures have gained such destructive control.

6. All of the documents take *the role of the church with utmost seriousness*. They write *as* committed church members in their own situation *to* church members elsewhere. Their basic orientation is not sociological or anthropological or "scientific," but ecclesiological and confessional. They feel that the church has a crucial role to play in the struggle for the *full* salvation of humankind—concern about the body as well as the soul—and that all Christians must be enlisted. They find that the struggle is not between the "good" church and the "evil" world, though there is clearly some of that; an even more crucial struggle is being waged *within the church* between proponents of the status quo and proponents of radical change. They agree with Augustine's assessment of the church: there are wolves within and sheep without. And they see even well-intentioned Christians "co-opting" the gospel so as to give sanction to unjust structures and seeking to destroy those who opt for change.

7. All of the documents, however, refuse to lay blame solely on the "others," acknowledging that *they themselves are complicit in wrongdoing*, and that along with all the "others" they must continually search out the evil in their own hearts, confess it, and ask God to empower them to do good rather than evil. (When one considers the centuries of oppression to which the people writing these documents have been subjected, this willingness to share responsibility is an indication of great spiritual maturity on the part of the writers.)

8. All of the documents, at the same time, seek to *"name the enemy,"* to locate the major sources of sin and destruction in their respective situations. To "name" the other, or to know the name of the other, is to begin to have power over it—a biblical insight with a long tradition. *Idolatry* is the name of the major enemy, the seductiveness of the worship of false gods even within the church, and false

gods elsewhere. They take many forms, from imperialism and colonialism to racism and the love of money, the last of which becomes a pervasive idol clothing itself in many forms.

9. All of the documents, despite the heaviness of the analysis, affirm *hope as the major contribution of the gospel.* It is a cause for wonder that this can be so pervasive in each document. In the midst of poverty, torture, malnutrition, warfare, and death, there is nevertheless a recognition that this is God's world, and that finally not even the worst that evil human beings can do will ultimately thwart God's purposes. Since God desires justice rather than injustice, and love rather than hate, this means that change is always possible; those who hope can be instruments for the fulfillment of God's intention.

10. All of the documents conclude *with great specificity in a variety of calls to action,* pointing to immediate and practical steps that need to be taken, by both the writers and readers of the documents. The calls to action save the documents from being mere cerebral exercises, and lead those who open themselves to the message to new depths of commitment and discipleship. Readers are not permitted the middle-class luxury of feeling immobilized by complexity, but can be energized by the single-mindedness of those who enlist in the struggle for justice for all people, not counting on their own efforts to save the world, but being assured that as they make themselves available, God will use their efforts in the fulfillment of God's own purposes.

Bracing Ourselves

The documents share one other characteristic that needs separate treatment: all of them are *exceedingly hard-hitting,* and with uncomfortable frequency their target is ourselves. This is least apparent (though implicitly clear) in the South African document. But lest we breathe too easily too soon, we discover that it is impossible to read its analyses of "state theology," "church theology," and "prophetic theology," without realizing that the descriptive framework mirrors our own situation in the United States with unflattering accuracy; we, too, have multiple counterparts of the first two positions, and only a scattered handful of the latter.

In the other documents, however, the finger is pointed explicitly at the United States of America, in its political, economic, and military postures, as a chief contributor to the outrages that have constituted life—and death—in Central America, South Africa and Asia. The analyses of our evil use of power in the past and the analyses of how we exploit and destroy human life in the present do not make pleasant reading, and there are certain paragraphs guaranteed to raise a lot of North American hackles, and ruffle a lot of beards. They deserve some equivalent of the most widely used phrase on American billboards: "Warning: the surgeon general has determined that reading these documents may be injurious to your psyche."

If that is so, some potential readers may ask, why should we subject ourselves to the cruel and unusual punishment of reading documents that attack us and our country? There are a number of reasons, however, why it is important not to close the book the first time we feel threatened or uncomfortable.

1. The source of the documents is important: these are the words of our sisters and brothers in Christ. If they were nothing but political tracts or sociological analyses, we might feel less obligated to stick with them. But when one part of the Christian community addresses itself to another part of that community, those addressed have a responsibility to listen.

2. The fact that the documents are written out of pain and suffering makes our listening to them not only desirable but mandatory. If someone is hurting, our first task is not to dissect the cry of pain in order to discredit it, but to take the cry seriously in order to respond to it. And if the cry not only goes, "We are hurting," but continues, ". . . and you, our brothers and sisters, are part of the reason we are hurting," then we have an obligation to respond in such a way that the pain can be healed.

3. The documents enable us to see the world through the eyes of others in ways that are not possible when we look at the world only through our own eyes. The writers of the documents see the human situation from an angle of vision denied to us, unless we are willing to see with them. It is important to see what they see, even if the spectacle is unpleasant—children victimized by malnutrition, men unable to find work, women forced into prostitution, dark-skinned peoples degraded, villages bombed, civilians tortured. The fact that (to put it gently) they see us as part of the problem rather than part

of the solution forces us to ask *why* they so perceive us; surely we abhor such things as much as they do. But (to put it less gently) the fact that they may be right about us, and not simply misperceiving the effects of our nation's deeds, is a fact to which we have to give at least initial credence. If they are right, then we must seek ways to repair whatever damage we have done, and set up new structures to make it impossible to do it in the future. On the other hand, if they have indeed misperceived us (at least in part), then together we must set the record straight.

5. The fact that we have so much power, and they have so little, is a final reason we must listen to them. Even if only a small part of what they say is true, it would still be the case that we are doing immense harm in the world with our military might, our economic domination, and our political arrogance. And just as they acknowledge that not all the evil in the world is being done by others, but that some of it is done by them, so we might come to acknowledge that if not all the evil is being done by us, a great deal of it *is* done by us, and that our obligation is to change that situation by changing ourselves. That process is called "conversion" in *The Road to Damascus,* and although we cannot convert ourselves, we can be open to letting God convert us and so transform our lives.

That is not the end of the road—even to Damascus—but it is a beginning.

The Kairos Document

Challenge to the Church

[South Africa]

Introduction

The Preface to *The Kairos Document* describes the circumstances of its creation: a critical situation in South Africa in June 1985 prompted a group of Christians to gather and reflect on what they needed to say and do, since silence would have represented complicity in evil. After much discussion and many meetings, various individuals and groups prepared drafts for a response, which itself was refined in further meetings, discussion, and redrafting. These results were then circulated to a yet wider group of individuals who were invited to respond to the "peoples' statement" by testing its fidelity to the biblical message. Throughout the process it was made clear that the document would remain open-ended, subject to ongoing review and refinement even after publication. Finally, a "Working Committee" synthesized these results in a draft that originally had over 150 signers from all walks of Christian life in South Africa. It was published on September 25, 1985. Thousands of people had been involved in its creation.

The response "generated more discussion and debate than any previous theological document in South Africa." There was so much interest that exactly one year later a second edition was issued, the text of which is reproduced below. It is similar to the initial draft save that the crucial Chapter Four, "Towards a Prophetic Theology," has been almost completely rewritten in the interests of clarity, in response to reactions to the first edition. Explanatory Notes were also added to clarify some initial misunderstandings and to deal more explicitly with the biblical basis of the document.

It is one of the virtues of the familiar Third World model of action-reflection-action-reflection that the process is never completed but remains open-ended, and *The Kairos Document* will continue to be revised as events in South Africa change.

Those or us who sit in comfortable surroundings and read texts should realize that when *The Kairos Document* was first released its signatories were putting their lives on the line; the government could have argued that the text constituted an act of treason punishable by death. The fact that there were no mass arrests, however, and the fact that since its publication South Africa has experienced extraordinary change attest both the timeliness and the substantive depth of the text itself.

The Kairos Document

Challenge to the Church

A Theological Comment on the
Political Crisis in South Africa

Revised Second Edition

Contents

Preface to the
Revised Second Edition

It is exactly one year since the publication of the first edition of *The Kairos Document*. At that time, we said that "South Africa has been plunged into a crisis that is shaking the foundations and *there is every indication that the crisis has only just begun* and that *it will deepen and become even more threatening in the months to come*". Today, one year later, the situation in South Africa is indeed far worse than before and the crisis far more serious.

A year ago we had a partial state of emergency, now we have a total, national state of emergency. Then one could, to a certain extent, report about what was happening in South Africa, now there is almost a total blackout of news. Then there were threats of sanctions, now it is a matter of what type of sanctions to apply against South Africa. There is more repression now than ever before with thousands of people in detention, many missing and some restricted or deported. Whilst the Botha regime is going all out to demonstrate its power and its determination to maintain apartheid at all costs, the people have become more determined than ever to resist this regime even at the cost of their lives. This is indeed frightening. It is a *real Kairos!*

The message of *The Kairos Document* has lost none of its relevance. If anything, it is more relevant today than it was a year ago.

The Kairos theologians have therefore decided to publish a second edition of the document.

After extensive discussions amongst the Kairos theologians and with regional groups around the country, and after considering all the contributions from various groups, churches and other persons here and abroad, and further, because of a desire to keep the document as simple as possible for easy reading by ordinary people, the editing of the document has been kept to a minimum. Amendments, elaborations and additions have been made only where it was absolutely necessary for greater clarity. We have tried to maintain the quality of the first edition, its mood, sharpness, vigor and simplicity, because this is what the signatories and others demanded. It had to be left as a prophetic word, a proclamation.

For this reason, no *debates* on the various themes raised by the first edition have been entered into. To meet this need the Kairos theologians are working on a book which will deal with the debates more scientifically. The publication of this book is scheduled for the middle of next year.

The only chapter of the original *Kairos Document* which has been almost completely rewritten is that on Prophetic Theology. It was generally felt that this chapter was not well developed in the first edition. Otherwise we have added explanatory notes to help clarify some of the points which were not clear. Also, because of the thousands of people who wanted to have their *names* put to the document, it has not been possible to include a list of signatories in this edition. It would have made the edition too voluminous. We are nevertheless keeping a record of the list.

Responses to the first edition were overwhelming. The document has generated more discussions and debates than any previous theological document in South Africa. There has been overwhelming excitement about it in the Black townships. It reinforced the people's faith and hope for a new and just society in South Africa. It came as an empowering instrument of faith committing them more than ever before to the struggle for justice and peace in South Africa. It was welcomed as a statement of what it means to be truly Christian in a violent apartheid society. For many, the Gospel became 'Good News' for the first time in their lives.

The document also had a mission dimension. Many of those who had abandoned the Church as an irrelevant institution that supports, justifies and legitimizes this cruel apartheid system began to feel that if the Church becomes the Church as expounded by *The Kairos Document* then they would go back to Church again. Even those who would consider themselves to be 'non-Christians' in the conventional sense began to say that if this is Christianity they could become Christians.

There have also been responses from some of the Churches in South Africa, from various Christian groups around the country and from individual theologians and various other persons. And we have received volumes of responses from our sister churches around the world. All were very helpful in advancing the development of an authentic and relevant theology that addresses itself to the issues of the day. Like any other challenging material the document has also been viciously attacked, mostly by conservative church groups like the 'Gospel Defence League' and 'Christian Mission International'. They actually called for the banning of the document. This came as no surprise to us as they are known for their support of the apartheid regime in South Africa and their attack on anyone who challenges this regime.

It might be interesting to study the relationship between the various individuals and groups who viciously attacked the document and those who welcomed it. For example, how does the theological stance relate to the class position or the social, economic, racial and political interests of these groups or individuals? What is clear is that most of those who attacked the document failed to appreciate the *concerns* of those who participated in producing the document. They looked at the document from their own situation or context, which is completely different from that of the participants whose experience and ministry come from the townships. Most of the critics simply took the document out of its context and analyzed it in the realm of abstraction.

To appreciate *The Kairos Document* one needs to understand and internalize the concerns of those who produced it. Those Christians who live in the townships and who are experiencing the civil war that is tearing their lives apart understand immediately what the Kairos theologians are attempting to say; whilst those who do not have this experience find it difficult to understand the document.

Perhaps the most exciting and important contribution of *The Kairos Document* has been its method or way of doing theology. Many Christians here and abroad are using the model or method of *The Kairos Document* to reflect on their own situation. They have begun to criticise the traditional, historical alignment of the Church with Western ideology, institutions and governments whilst those in the East are grappling with the question of how to live one's faith in socialist societies.

Against this background we publish today this second edition of *The Kairos Document*. It was developed in the same way as the first edition except that thousands of people have been involved in the process, not only in terms of reflection and study but mostly in terms of involvement and action in the liberation struggle in South Africa. We hope that this edition will not be the end of the process of action and theological reflection on our situation. We hope that it will serve as a never-ending stimulus to keep the cycle of action-reflection-action moving forward.

September 1986

Preface

The KAIROS Document is a Christian, biblical and theological comment on the political crisis in South Africa today. It is an attempt by concerned Christians in South Africa to reflect on the situation of death in our country. It is a critique of the current theological models that determine the type of activities the Church engages in to try to resolve the problems of the country. It is an attempt to develop, out of this perplexing situation, an alternative biblical and theological model that will in turn lead to forms of activity that will make a real difference to the future of our country.

Of particular interest is *the way* the theological material was produced. In June 1985 as the crisis was intensifying in the country, as more and more people were killed, maimed and imprisoned, as one Black township after another revolted against the apartheid regime, as the people refused to be oppressed or to cooperate with oppressors, facing death by the day, and as the apartheid army moved into the townships to rule by the barrel of the gun, a number of theologians who were concerned about the situation expressed the need to reflect on this situation to determine what response by the Church and by all Christians in South Africa would be most appropriate.

A first discussion group met at the beginning of July in the heart of Soweto. Participants spoke freely about the situation and the various responses of the Church, Church leaders and Christians. A critique of these responses was made and the theology from which these responses flowed was also subjected to a critical analysis. Individual members of the group were assigned to put together material on specific themes which were raised during the discussion and to present the material to the next session of the group.

At the second meeting the material itself was subjected to a critique and various people were commissioned to do more investigations on specific problematic areas. The latest findings with the rest of the material were collated and presented to the third meeting where more than thirty people, consisting of theologians, ordinary Christians (lay theologians) and some Church leaders came together.

After a very extensive discussion some adjustments and additions were made especially in regard to the section entitled 'Challenge to Action'. The group then appointed a committee to subject the document to further critique by various other Christian groupings throughout the country. Everybody was told that "this was a people's document which you can also own even by demolishing it if your position can stand the test of biblical faith and Christian experience in South Africa". They were told that this was an open-ended document which will never be said to be final.

The 'Working Committee', as it was called, was inundated with comments, suggestions and enthusiastic appreciation from various groups and individuals in the country. By the 13th September 1985 when the document was submitted for publication there were still comments and recommendations flowing in. The first publication therefore must be taken as a beginning, a basis for further discussion by all Christians in the country. Further editions will be published later.

25 September 1985
Johannesburg

CHAPTER ONE

The Moment of Truth

The time has come. The moment of truth has arrived. South Africa has been plunged into a crisis that is shaking the foundations and there is every indication that the crisis has only just begun and that it will deepen and become even more threatening in the months to come. It is the KAIROS[1] or moment of truth not only for apartheid but also for the Church and all other faiths and religions.[2]

We as a group of theologians have been trying to understand the theological significance of this moment in our history. It is serious, very serious. For very many Christians in South Africa this is the KAIROS, the moment of grace and opportunity, the favourable time in which God issues a challenge to decisive action. It is a dangerous time because, if this opportunity is missed, and allowed to pass by, the loss for the Church, for the Gospel and for all the people of South Africa will be immeasurable. Jesus wept over Jerusalem. He wept over the tragedy of the destruction of the city and the massacre of the

---

1. Kairos is the Greek word that is used in the Bible to designate a special moment of time when God visits his people to offer them a unique opportunity for repentance and conversion, for change and decisive action. It is a time of judgment. It is a moment of truth, a crisis. (See, for example, Mk 1:15; 13:33; Lk 8:13; 19:44; Rom 13:11-13; I Cor 7:29; II Cor 6:2; Tit 1:3; Rev 1:3; 22:10.)

2. What is said here of Christianity and the Church could be applied, *mutatis mutandis,* to other faiths and religions in South Africa; but this particular document is addressed to "all who bear the name Christian" (see Conclusion).

people that was imminent, "and all because you did not recognise your opportunity (KAIROS) when God offered it" (Lk 19:44).

A crisis is a judgment that brings out the best in some people and the worst in others. A crisis is a moment of truth that shows us up for what we really are. There will be no place to hide and no way of pretending to be what we are not in fact. At this moment in South Africa the Church is about to be shown up for what it really is and no cover-up will be possible.

What the present crisis shows up, although many of us have known it all along, is that *the Church is divided.* More and more people are now saying that there are in fact two Churches in South Africa—a White Church and a Black Church. Even within the same denomination there are in fact two Churches. In the life and death conflict between different social forces that has come to a head in South Africa today, there are Christians (or at least people who profess to be Christians) on both sides of the conflict—and some who are trying to sit on the fence!

Does this prove that Christian faith has no real meaning or relevance for our times? Does it show that the Bible can be used for any purpose at all? Such problems would be critical enough for the Church in any circumstances, but when we also come to see that the conflict in South Africa is between the oppressor and the oppressed,[3] the crisis for the Church as an institution becomes much more acute.[4] Both oppressor and oppressed claim loyalty to the same Church. They are both baptised in the same baptism and participate together in the breaking of the same bread, the same body and blood of Christ. There we sit in the same Church while outside Christian policemen and soldiers are beating up and killing Christian children or torturing Christian prisoners to death while yet other Christians stand by and weakly plead for peace.

The Church is divided against itself[5] and its day of judgment has come.

---

3. See Chapter Four below.

4. If the apostle Paul judged that the truth of the gospel was at stake when Greek and Jewish Christians no longer ate together (Gal 2:11-14), how much more acute is the crisis for the gospel of Jesus Christ when some Christians take part in the systematic oppression of other Christians!

5. Mt 12:25; I Cor 1:13.

The moment of truth has compelled us to analyse more carefully the different theologies in our Churches and to speak out more clearly and boldly about the real significance of these theologies. We have been able to isolate three theologies, and we have chosen to call them 'State Theology', 'Church Theology' and 'Prophetic Theology'.[6] In our thoroughgoing criticism of the first and second theologies we do not wish to mince our words. The situation is too critical for that.

6. These are obviously not the only theologies that are current in South Africa, but they represent the three Christian theological stances in relation to the present situation in South Africa.

CHAPTER TWO

Critique of 'State Theology'

The South African apartheid State has a theology of its own, and we have chosen to call it 'State Theology'. 'State Theology' is simply the theological justification of the status quo with its racism, capitalism and totalitarianism. It blesses injustice, canonises the will of the powerful and reduces the poor to passivity, obedience and apathy.[7]

How does 'State Theology' do this? It does it by misusing theological concepts and biblical texts for its own political purposes. In this document we would like to draw your attention to four key examples of how this is done in South Africa. The first would be the use of Romans 13:1-7 to give an absolute and 'divine' authority to the State. The second would be the use of the idea of 'Law and Order' to determine and control what the people may be permitted to regard as just and unjust. The third would be the use of the word 'communist' to brand anyone who rejects 'State Theology'. And finally there is the use that is made of the name of God.

---

7. What we are referring to here is something more than the 'Apartheid Theology' of the White Dutch Reformed Churches that once tried to justify apartheid by appealing to certain texts in the Bible. Our analysis of present-day theological stances has led us to the conclusion that there is a 'State Theology' that does not only justify racism but justifies all the activities of the State in its attempts to hold on to power and that is subscribed to as a theology well beyond the White Dutch Reformed Churches.

2.1 Romans 13:1-7

The text reads as follows:

> 1. You must all obey the governing authorities. Since all government comes from God, the civil authorities were appointed by God.
> 2. And so anyone who resists authority is rebelling against God's decision, and such an act is bound to be punished.
> 3. Good behaviour is not afraid of magistrates; only criminals have anything to fear. If you want to live without being afraid of authority, you must live honestly and authority may even honour you.
> 4. The State is there to serve God for your benefit. If you break the law, however, you may well have fear: the bearing of the sword has its significance. The authorities are there to serve God: they carry out God's revenge by punishing wrongdoers.
> 5. You must obey, therefore, not only because you are afraid of being punished, but also for conscience' sake.
> 6. This is also the reason why you must pay taxes, since all government officials are God's officers. They serve God by collecting taxes.
> 7. Pay every government official what he has a right to ask—whether it be direct tax or indirect, fear or honour. (Rom 13:1-7)[8]

The misuse of this famous text is not confined to the present government in South Africa. Throughout the history of Christianity totalitarian regimes have tried to legitimise an attitude of blind obedience and absolute servility towards the State by quoting this text. "As soon as Christians, out of loyalty to the gospel of Jesus, offer resistance to a State's totalitarian claim, the representatives of the State or their collaborationist theological advisers are accustomed to appeal to this saying of Paul, as if Christians are here commended to endorse and thus to abet all the crimes of a totalitarian State."[9]

---

8. This and all other quotations in this document are taken from the Jerusalem Bible. The reader is invited to compare this translation with others that he or she might prefer.

9. Oscar Cullmann, *The State in the New Testament,* SCM, 1957, p. 56.

But what then is the meaning of Rom 13:1-7 and why is the use made of it by 'State Theology' unjustifiable from a biblical point of view?

'State Theology' assumes that in this text Paul is presenting us with the absolute and definitive Christian doctrine about the State, in other words an absolute and universal principle that is equally valid for all times and in all circumstances. The falseness of this assumption has been pointed out by numerous biblical scholars.[10]

What has been overlooked here is one of the most fundamental of all principles of biblical interpretation: every text must be interpreted *in its context*. To abstract a text from its context and to interpret it in the abstract is to distort the meaning of God's Word. Moreover, the context here is not only the chapters and verses that precede and succeed this particular text, nor is it even limited to the total context of the Bible. The context includes also the *circumstances* in which Paul's statement was made. Paul was writing to a particular Christian community in Rome, a community that had its own particular problems in relation to the State at that time and in those circumstances. That is part of the context of our text.

Many authors have drawn attention to the fact that in the rest of the Bible God does not demand obedience to oppressive rulers. Examples can be given ranging from Pharaoh to Pilate and through into Apostolic times. The Jews and later the Christians did not believe that their imperial overlords, the Egyptians, the Babylonians, the Greeks or the Romans, had some kind of divine right to rule them and oppress them. These empires were the beasts described in the Book of Daniel and the Book of Revelation. God *allowed* them to rule for a while, but he did not *approve* of what they did. It was not God's will. His will was the freedom and liberation of Israel. Rom 13:1-7 cannot be contradicting all of this.

But most revealing of all is the circumstances of the Roman Christians to whom Paul was writing. They were not revolutionaries. They were not trying to overthrow the State. They were not calling for a change of government. They were what has been called 'antinomians' or 'enthusiasts', and their belief was that Christians, and

---

10. For example: E. Käsemann, *Commentary on Romans,* Eerdmans, 1980, pp. 354-57; O. Cullmann, op. cit., pp. 55-57.

only Christians, were exonerated from obeying any State at all, any government or political authority at all, because Jesus alone was their Lord and King. This is of course heretical, and Paul is compelled to point out to these Christians that before the second coming of Christ there will always be some kind of State, some kind of secular government, and that Christians are not exonerated from subjection to some kind of political authority.

Paul is simply not addressing the issue of a just or unjust State or the need to change one government for another. He is simply establishing the fact that there will be some kind of secular authority and that Christians as such are not exonerated from subjection to secular laws and authorities. *"The State is there to serve God for your benefit"*, says Paul. That is the kind of State he is speaking of. That is the kind of State that must be obeyed. In this text Paul does not tell us what we should do when a State does *not* serve God and does *not* work for the benefit of all but has become unjust and oppressive. That is another question.

If we wish to search the Bible for guidance in a situation where the State that is supposed to be "the servant of God" betrays that calling and begins to serve Satan instead, then we can study chapter 13 of the Book of Revelation. Here the Roman State becomes the servant of the dragon (the devil) and takes on the appearance of a horrible beast. Its days are numbered because God will not permit his unfaithful servant to reign forever.

Consequently those who try to find answers to the very different questions and problems of our time in the text of Rom 13:1-7 are doing a great disservice to Paul. The use that 'State Theology' makes of this text tells us more about the political options of those who construct this theology than it does about the meaning of God's Word in this text. As one biblical scholar puts it: "The primary concern is to justify the interests of the State and the text is pressed into its service without respect for the context and the intention of Paul".

2.2 Law and Order

The State makes use of the concept of law and order to maintain the status quo which it depicts as 'normal'. But this *law* is the unjust and discriminatory laws of apartheid, and this *order* is the organised and institutionalised disorder of oppression. Any who wish to change this law and this order are made to feel lawless and disorderly or, in other words, guilty of sin.

It is indeed the duty of the State to maintain law and order, but it has no divine mandate to maintain any kind of law and order. Something does not become moral and just simply because the State has declared it to be a law, and the organisation of a society is not a just and right order simply because it has been instituted by the State. We cannot accept any kind of law and any kind of order. The concern of Christians is that we should have in our country a just law and a right order.

In the present crisis and especially during the State of Emergency, 'State Theology' has tried to reestablish the status quo of orderly discrimination, exploitation and oppression by appealing to the consciences of its citizens in the name of law and order. It tries to make those who reject this law and this order feel that they are ungodly. The State here is not only usurping the right of the Church to make judgments about what would be right and just in our circumstances; it is going even further than that and demanding of us, in the name of law and order, an obedience that must be reserved for God alone. The South African State recognises no authority beyond itself, and therefore it will not allow anyone to question what it has chosen to define as 'law and order'. However, there are millions of Christians in South Africa today who are saying with Peter: "We must obey God rather than man (human beings)" (Acts 5:29).

'State Theology' further believes that the government has the God-given right to use *violence* to enforce its system of 'law and order'. It bases this on Romans 13:4: 'The authorities are there to serve God: they carry out God's revenge by punishing wrongdoers'. In this way *state security* becomes a more important concern than *justice*, and those who in the name of God work to change the unjust structures of society are branded as ungodly agitators and rebels. The State often admonishes church leaders to 'preach the pure gospel' and not to 'meddle in politics', while at the same time it indulges in its own political theology which claims God's approval for its use of violence in maintaining an unjust system of 'law and order'.

The State appeals to the consciences of Christians in the name of 'law and order' to accept this use of violence as a God-given duty, in order to reestablish the status quo of oppression. In this way people are sacrificed for the sake of laws, rather than laws for the sake of people, as in the life of Jesus: 'The sabbath was made for man (the human person); not man (the human person) for the sabbath' (Mark 2:27). The State's efforts to preserve law and order, which should imply the protection of human life, mean the very opposite for the majority of the people, namely the suppression and destruction of life.

2.3 The Threat of Communism

We all know how the South African State makes use of the label 'communist'. Anything that threatens the status quo is labelled 'communist'. Anyone who opposes the State and especially anyone who rejects its theology is simply dismissed as a 'communist'. No account is taken of what communism really means. No thought is given to why some people have indeed opted for communism or for some form of socialism. Even people who have not rejected capitalism are called 'communists' when they reject 'State Theology'. The State uses the label 'communist' in an uncritical and unexamined way as its symbol of evil.

'State Theology', like every other theology, needs to have its own concrete symbol of evil. It must be able to symbolise what it regards as godless behaviour and what ideas must be regarded as atheistic. It must have its own version of hell. And so it has invented, or rather taken over, the myth of communism. All evil is communistic, and all communist or socialist ideas are atheistic and godless. Threats about hell-fire and eternal damnation are replaced by threats and warnings about the horrors of a tyrannical, totalitarian, atheistic and terrorist communist regime—a kind of hell-on-earth. This is a very convenient way of frightening some people into accepting any kind of domination and exploitation by a capitalist minority.

The South African State has its own heretical theology, and according to that theology millions of Christians in South Africa (not to mention the rest of the world) are to be regarded as 'atheists'. It is significant that in earlier times when Christians rejected the gods of the Roman Empire they were branded as 'atheists'—by the State.

2.4 The God of the State

The State in its oppression of the people makes use again and again of the name of God. Military chaplains use it to encourage the South African Defence Force, police chaplains use it to strengthen police-men and cabinet ministers use it in their propaganda speeches. But perhaps the most revealing of all is the blasphemous use of God's holy name in the preamble to the new apartheid constitution.

> In humble submission to Almighty God, who controls the desti-nies of nations and the history of peoples who gathered our forebears together from many lands and gave them this their own; who has guided them from generation to generation; who has wondrously delivered them from the dangers that beset them.

This god is an idol. It is as mischievous, sinister and evil as any of the idols that the prophets of Israel had to contend with. Here we have a god who is historically on the side of the white settlers, who dispossesses black people of their land and who gives the major part of the land to his "chosen people".

It is the god of superior weapons who conquered those who were armed with nothing but spears. It is the god of the casspirs and hippos, the god of tear gas, rubber bullets, sjamboks, prison cells and death sentences. Here is a god who exalts the proud and humbles the poor—the very opposite of the God of the Bible who "scatters the proud of heart, pulls down the mighty from their thrones and exalts the humble" (Lk 1:51-52). From a theological point of view the opposite of the God of the Bible is the devil, Satan. The god of the South African State is not merely an idol or false god, it is the devil disguised as Almighty God—the antichrist.

The oppressive South African regime will always be particularly abhorrent to Christians precisely because it makes use of Christianity to justify its evil ways. As Christians we simply cannot tolerate this blasphemous use of God's name and God's Word. 'State Theology' is not only heretical, it is blasphemous. Christians who are trying to remain faithful to the God of the Bible are even more horrified when they see that there are Churches, like the White Dutch Reformed

Churches and other groups of Christians, who actually subscribe to this heretical theology. 'State Theology' needs its own prophets, and it manages to find them from the ranks of those who profess to be ministers of God's Word in some of our Churches. What is particularly tragic for a Christian is to see the number of people who are fooled and confused by these false prophets and their heretical theology.

South African 'State Theology' can be compared with the 'Court Theology' of Israel's Kings, and our false prophets can be compared with the 'Court Prophets' of Israel, of whom it is said:

> 'They have misled my people by saying: Peace! when there is no peace. Instead of my people rebuilding the wall, these men come and slap on plaster. I mean to shatter the wall you slapped with plaster, to throw it down and lay its foundations bare. It will fall and you will perish under it; and so you will learn that I am Yahweh' (Ezekiel 13:10, 14).

CHAPTER THREE

Critique of 'Church Theology'

We have analysed the statements that are made from time to time by the so-called 'English-speaking' Churches. We have looked at what Church leaders tend to say in their speeches and press statements about the apartheid regime and the present crisis. What we found running through all these pronouncements is a series of interrelated theological assumptions. These we have chosen to call 'Church Theology'. We are well aware of the fact that this theology does *not* express the faith of the majority of Christians in South Africa today who form the greater part of most of our Churches. Nevertheless the opinions expressed by Church leaders are regarded in the media and generally in our society as the official opinions of the Churches.[11] We have therefore chosen to call these opinions 'Church Theology'. The crisis in which we find ourselves today compels us to question this theology, to question its assumptions, its implications and its practicality.

In a limited, guarded and cautious way this theology is critical of apartheid. Its criticism, however, is superficial and counterproduc-

---

11. We realise only too well that we are making broad and sweeping generalisations here. There are some Church statements that would be exceptions to this general tendency. However, what concerns us here is that there is a set of opinions that in the mind of the people are associated with the liberal 'English-speaking' Churches.

tive because instead of engaging in an in-depth analysis of the signs of our times, it relies upon a few stock ideas derived from Christian tradition and then uncritically and repeatedly applies them to our situation. The stock ideas used by almost all these Church leaders that we would like to examine here are: reconciliation (or peace), justice and nonviolence.

3.1 Reconciliation

There can be no doubt that our Christian faith commits us to work for *true* reconciliation and *genuine* peace. But as so many people, including Christians, have pointed out, there can be no true reconciliation and no genuine peace *without justice*. Any form of peace or reconciliation that allows the sin of injustice and oppression to continue is a *false* peace and *counterfeit* reconciliation. This kind of "reconciliation" has nothing whatsoever to do with the Christian faith.

"Church Theology" is not always clear on this matter, and many Christians have been led to believe that what we need in South Africa is not justice but reconciliation and peace. The argument goes something like this: "We must be fair. We must listen to both sides of the story. If the two sides can only meet to talk and negotiate they will sort out their differences and misunderstandings, and the conflict will be resolved". On the face of it this may sound very Christian. But is it?

The fallacy here is that 'reconciliation' has been made into an absolute principle that must be applied in all cases of conflict or dissension. But not all cases of conflict are the same. We can imagine a private quarrel between two people or two groups whose differences are based upon misunderstandings. In such cases it would be appropriate to talk and negotiate to sort out the misunderstandings and to reconcile the two sides. But there are other conflicts in which one side is right and the other wrong. There are conflicts where one side is a fully armed and violent oppressor while the other side is defenceless and oppressed. There are conflicts that can only be described as the struggle between justice and injustice, good and evil, God and the devil. To speak of reconciling these two is not only a mistaken application of the Christian idea of reconciliation, it is a total betrayal of all that Christian faith has ever meant. Nowhere in the Bible or in Christian tradition has it ever been suggested that we ought to try to reconcile good and evil, God and the devil. We are supposed to do away with evil, injustice, oppression and sin—not come to terms with it. We are supposed to oppose, confront and reject the devil and not try to sup with the devil.

In our situation in South Africa today it would be totally un-Christian to plead for reconciliation and peace before the present injustices have been removed. Any such plea plays into the hands of the oppressor by trying to persuade those of us who are oppressed to accept our oppression and to become reconciled to the intolerable crimes that are committed against us. That is not Christian reconciliation, it is sin. It is asking us to become accomplices in our own oppression, to become servants of the devil. No reconciliation is possible in South Africa *without justice,* without the total dismantling of apartheid.

What this means in practice is that no reconciliation, no forgiveness and no negotiations are possible *without repentance.* The biblical teaching on reconciliation and forgiveness makes it quite clear that nobody can be forgiven and reconciled with God unless she or he repents of their sins. Nor are *we* expected to forgive the unrepentant sinner. When he or she repents we must be willing to forgive seventy times seven times, but before that we are expected to preach repentance to those who sin against us or against anyone. Reconciliation, forgiveness and negotiations will become our Christian duty in South Africa only when the apartheid regime shows signs of genuine repentance.[12] The recent State of Emergency, the continued military repres-

---

12. It should be noted here that there is a difference between the willingness to forgive, on the one hand, and the reality of forgiveness or the experience of being forgiven with all its healing consequences, on the other hand. God's forgiveness is unconditional and permanent in the sense that he is always *willing to forgive.* Jesus expresses this on the cross by saying, "Father, forgive them, for they know not what they do" (Lk 23:34). However, we as sinners will not experience God's forgiveness in our lives, we will not actually be freed or liberated from our sins, until we confess and renounce our sins (I Jn 1:8-9) and until we demonstrate the fruits of repentance (Lk 3:7-14).

Human beings must also be *willing to forgive* one another at all times, even seventy times seven times. But forgiveness will not become a reality with all its healing effects until the offender repents. Thus in South Africa forgiveness will

sion of the people in the townships and the jailing of all its opponents, is clear proof of the total lack of repentance on the part of the present regime.

There is nothing that we want more than true reconciliation and genuine peace—the peace that God wants and not the peace the world wants (Jn 14:27). The peace that God wants is based upon truth, repentance, justice and love. The peace that the world offers us is a unity that compromises the truth, covers over injustice and oppression and is totally motivated by selfishness. At this stage, like Jesus, we must expose this false peace, confront our oppressors and be prepared for the dissension that will follow. As Christians we must say with Jesus: "Do you suppose that I am here to bring peace on earth. No, I tell you, but rather dissension" (Lk 12:51). There can be no real peace without justice and repentance.

It would be quite wrong to try to preserve 'peace' and 'unity' at all costs, even at the cost of truth and justice and, worse still, at the cost of thousands of young lives. As disciples of Jesus we should rather promote truth and justice and life at all costs, even at the cost of creating conflict, disunity and dissension along the way. To be truly biblical our Church leaders must adopt a theology that millions of Christians have already adopted—a biblical theology of direct confrontation with the forces of evil rather than a theology of reconciliation with sin and the devil.

3.2 Justice

It would be quite wrong to give the impression that 'Church Theology' in South Africa is not particularly concerned about the need for justice. There have been some very strong and very sincere demands for justice. But the question we need to ask here, the very serious theo-

---

not become an experienced reality until the apartheid regime shows signs of genuine repentance. Our willingness to forgive must not be taken to mean a willingness to allow sin to continue, a willingness to allow our oppressors to continue oppressing us. To ask us to forgive our unrepentant oppressors in the sense that we simply ignore or overlook the fact that they are continuing to humiliate, crush, repress, imprison, maim and kill us is to add insult to injury.

What is required at this stage above all else is repentance and conversion.

logical question is: What kind of justice? An examination of Church statements and pronouncements gives the distinct impression that the justice that is envisaged is *the justice of reform,* that is to say, a justice that is determined by the oppressor, by the white minority and that is offered to the people as a kind of concession. It does not appear to be the more radical justice that comes from below and is determined by the people of South Africa.

One of our main reasons for drawing this conclusion is the simple fact that almost all Church statements and appeals are made to the State or to the white community. The assumption seems to be that changes must come from whites or at least from people who are at the top of the pile. The general idea appears to be that one must simply appeal to the conscience and the goodwill of those who are responsible for injustice in our land and that once they have repented of their sins and after some consultation with others they will introduce the necessary reforms to the system. Why else would Church leaders be having talks with P W Botha, if this is not the vision of a just and peaceful solution to our problems?

At the heart of this approach is the reliance upon 'individual conversions' in response to 'moralising demands' to change the structures of a society. It has not worked, and it never will work. The present crisis with all its cruelty, brutality and callousness is ample proof of the ineffectiveness of years and years of Christian 'moralising' about the need for love. The problem that we are dealing with here in South Africa is not merely a problem of personal guilt, it is a problem of structural injustice. People are suffering, people are being maimed and killed and tortured every day. We cannot just sit back and wait for the oppressor to see the light so that the oppressed can put out their hands and beg for the crumbs of some small reforms. That in itself would be degrading and oppressive.

There have been reforms and, no doubt, there will be further reforms in the near future. And it may well be that the Church's appeal to the consciences of whites has contributed marginally to the introduction of some of these reforms. But can such reforms ever be regarded as real change, as the introduction of a true and lasting justice? Reforms that come from the top are never satisfactory. They seldom do more than make the oppression more effective and more acceptable. If the oppressor does ever introduce reforms that might lead to real change, this will come about because of strong pressure from those who are oppressed. True justice, God's justice, demands a radical change of structures. This can only come from below, from the oppressed themselves. God will bring about change through the oppressed as he did through the oppressed Hebrew slaves in Egypt. God does not bring his justice through reforms introduced by the Pharaohs of this world.[13]

Why then does 'Church Theology' appeal to the top rather than to the people who are suffering? Why does this theology not demand that the oppressed stand up for their rights and wage a struggle against their oppressors? Why does it not tell them that it is *their* duty to work for justice and to change the unjust structures? Perhaps the answer to these questions is that appeals from the 'top' in the Church tend very easily to be appeals to the 'top' in society. An appeal to the conscience of those who perpetuate the system of injustice must be made. But real change and true justice can only come from below, from the people—most of whom are Christians.

---

13. Despite what is clearly stated here in the text, several commentators have interpreted the concept of "justice from below" as an exclusion of God and an exclusion of the people who are now at the top. This misinterpretation is very revealing. In the first place it assumes that *God belongs on top* together with the kings, rulers, governments and others who have power, whether they are oppressors or not, and that God cannot work *from below,* through the efforts of the people who are oppressed. It assumes that God is on the side of the oppressor (on top) and not on the side of the oppressed (below). This is precisely what *The Kairos Document* is contesting.

In the second place there is the conclusion that "justice from below" excludes the White community and anyone else who is presently on top. This is based upon the very revealing assumption that conversion and repentance are impossible and that those who are presently on top will never climb down in order to negotiate as equals with those who are presently at the bottom. Unless they do this, they will indeed be unable to be part of the construction of a just and peaceful South Africa. Those who refuse to repent and change cannot become instruments of God's justice and God's peace.

3.3 Nonviolence

The stance of 'Church Theology' on nonviolence, expressed as a blanket condemnation of all that is *called* violence, has not only been unable to curb the violence of our situation, it has actually, although unwittingly, been a major contributing factor in the recent escalation of State violence. Here again nonviolence has been made into an absolute principle that applies to anything anyone *calls* violence without regard for who is using it, which side they are on or what purpose they may have in mind. In our situation, this is simply counterproductive.

The problem for the Church here is the way the word *violence* is being used in the propaganda of the State. The State and the media have chosen to call violence what some people do in the townships as they struggle for their liberation, that is, throwing stones, burning cars and buildings and sometimes killing collaborators. But this *excludes* the structural, institutional and unrepentant violence of the State and especially the oppressive and naked violence of the police and the army. These things are not counted as violence. And even when they are acknowledged to be 'excessive', they are called 'misconduct' or even 'atrocities' but never violence. Thus the phrase 'violence in the townships' comes to mean what the young people are doing and not what the police are doing or what apartheid in general is doing to people. If one calls for nonviolence in such circumstances one appears to be criticising the resistance of the people while justifying or at least overlooking the violence of the police and the State. That is how it is understood not only by the State and its supporters but also by the people who are struggling for their freedom. Violence, especially in our circumstances, is a loaded word.

It is true that Church statements and pronouncements do also condemn the violence of the police. They do say that they condemn *all violence.* But is it legitimate, especially in our circumstances, to use the same word *violence* in a blanket condemnation to cover the ruthless and repressive activities of the State and the desperate attempts of the people to defend themselves? Do such abstractions and generalisations not confuse the issue? How can acts of oppression, injustice and domination be equated with acts of resistance and self-defence? Would it be legitimate to describe both the physical force used by a rapist and the physical force used by a woman trying to resist the rapist as violence?

Moreover, there is nothing in the Bible or in our Christian tradition that would permit us to make such generalisations. Throughout the Bible the word violence is used to describe everything that is done by a wicked oppressor (for example, Ps 72:12-14; Is 59:1-8; Jer 22:13-17; Amos 3:9-10; 6:3; Mic 2:2; 3:1-3; 6:12). It is never used to describe the activities of Israel's armies in attempting to liberate themselves or to resist aggression. When Jesus says that we should turn the other cheek he is telling us that we must not take revenge; he is not saying that we should never defend ourselves or others. There is a long and consistent Christian tradition about the use of physical force to defend oneself against aggressors and tyrants. In other words, there are circumstances when physical force may be used. They are very restrictive circumstances, only as the very last resort and only as the lesser of two evils, or, as Bonhoeffer put it, "the lesser of two guilts". But it is simply not true to say that every possible use of physical force is violence and that no matter what the circumstances may be it is never permissible.

This is not to say that any use of force at any time by people who are oppressed is permissible simply because they are struggling for their liberation. There have been cases of killing and maiming that no Christian would want to approve of. But then our disapproval is based upon a concern for genuine liberation and a conviction that such acts are unnecessary, counterproductive and unjustifiable and not because they fall under a blanket condemnation of any use of physical force in any circumstances.

And finally what makes the professed nonviolence of 'Church Theology' extremely suspect in the eyes of very many people, including ourselves, is the tacit support that many Church leaders give to the growing *militarisation* of the South African State. How can one condemn all violence and then appoint chaplains to a very violent and oppressive army? How can one condemn all violence and then allow young white males to accept their conscription into the armed forces? Is it because the activities of the armed forces and the police are counted as defensive? That raises very serious questions about whose side such Church leaders might be on. Why are the activities of young blacks in the townships not regarded as defensive?

The problem of the Church here is that it starts from the premise that the apartheid regime in South Africa is a *legitimate authority*. It ignores the fact that it is a white minority regime which has imposed itself upon the majority of the people, that is blacks, in this country, that it maintains itself by brutality and violent force and that a majority of South Africans regard this regime as illegitimate.

In practice what one calls 'violence' and what one calls 'self-defence' seem to depend upon which side one is on. To call all physical force 'violence' is to try to be neutral and to refuse to make a judgment about who is right and who is wrong. The attempt to remain neutral in this kind of conflict is futile. Neutrality enables the status quo of oppression (and therefore violence) to continue. It is a way of giving tacit support to the oppressor, a support for brutal violence.[14]

3.4 The Fundamental Problem

It is not enough to criticise 'Church Theology'; we must also try to account for it. What is behind the mistakes and misunderstandings and inadequacies of this theology?

In the first place we can point to a lack of *social analysis*. We have seen how 'Church Theology' tends to make use of absolute principles like reconciliation, negotiation, nonviolence and peaceful solutions and applies them indiscriminately and uncritically to all situations. Very little attempt is made to analyse what is actually happening in our society and why it is happening. It is not possible to make valid moral judgments about a society without first understanding that society. The analysis of apartheid that underpins 'Church Theology' is simply inadequate. The present crisis has now made it very clear that the efforts of Church leaders to promote effective and practical ways of changing our society have failed. This failure is due in no small measure to the fact that 'Church Theology' has not

---

14. What we have said here about violence and nonviolence does not pretend to be a solution to the complex moral problems that we are all faced with as our country is plunged more and deeply into civil war. Our only aim in this section has been to critique an oversimplified and misleading theology of nonviolence.

developed a social analysis that would enable it to understand the mechanics of injustice and oppression.

Closely linked to this is the lack in 'Church Theology' of an adequate understanding of politics and *political strategy*. Changing the structures of a society is fundamentally a matter of politics. It requires a political strategy based upon a clear social or political analysis. The Church has to address itself to these strategies and to the analysis upon which they are based. It is into this political situation that the Church has to bring the gospel. Not as an alternative solution to our problems as if the gospel provided us with a nonpolitical solution to political problems. There is no specifically Christian solution. There will be a Christian way of approaching the political solutions, a Christian spirit and motivation and attitude. But there is no way of bypassing politics and political strategies.

But we have still not pinpointed the fundamental problem. Why has 'Church Theology' not developed a social analysis? Why does it have an inadequate understanding of the need for political strategies? And why does it make a virtue of neutrality and sitting on the sidelines?

The answer must be sought in the *type of faith and spirituality* that has dominated Church life for centuries. As we all know, spirituality has tended to be an otherworldly affair that has very little, if anything at all, to do with the affairs of this world. Social and political matters were seen as worldly affairs that have nothing to do with the spiritual concerns of the Church. Moreover, spirituality has also been understood to be purely private and individualistic. Public affairs and social problems were thought to be beyond the sphere of spirituality. And finally the spirituality we inherit tends to rely upon God to intervene in God's own good time to put right what is wrong in the world. That leaves very little for human beings to do except to pray for God's intervention.

It is precisely this kind of spirituality that, when faced with the present crisis in South Africa, leaves so many Christians and Church leaders in a state of near paralysis.

It hardly needs saying that this kind of faith and this type of spirituality has no biblical foundation. The Bible does not separate the human person from the world in which he or she lives; it does not separate the individual from the social or one's private life from one's public life. God redeems the whole person as part of God's whole creation (Rom 8:18-24). A truly biblical spirituality would penetrate into every aspect of human existence and would exclude nothing from God's redemptive will. Biblical faith is prophetically relevant to everything that happens in the world.

CHAPTER FOUR

Towards a Prophetic Theology

Our present KAIROS calls for a response from Christians that is biblical, spiritual, pastoral and, above all, prophetic. *What is it then that would make our response truly prophetic? What would be the characteristics of a prophetic theology?*[15]

---

15. Many readers of the first edition suggested that the meaning of prophetic theology should be spelt out more clearly. The characteristics of prophetic theology that have been included in this second edition are a summary of discussions among Kairos theologians both before and immediately after the publication of the first edition.

It should also be noted that there is a subtle difference between prophetic theology and people's theology. *The Kairos Document* itself, signed by theologians, ministers and other church workers, and addressed to all who bear the name Christian, is a prophetic statement. But the process that led to the production of the document, the process of theological reflection and action in groups, the involvement of many different people in doing theology was an exercise in people's theology. The document is therefore pointing out two things: that our present Kairos challenges Church leaders and others Christians to speak out prophetically and that our present Kairos is challenging all of us to do theology together reflecting upon our experiences in working for justice and peace in South Africa and thereby developing together a better theological understanding of our Kairos. The method that was used to produce *The Kairos Document* shows that theology is not the preserve of professional theologians, ministers and priests. Ordinary Christians can participate in theological reflection and should be encouraged to do so. When this people's theology is proclaimed to others to challenge and inspire them, it takes on the character of a prophetic theology.

4.1 Prophetic Theology

To be truly prophetic, our response would have to be, in the first place, solidly grounded in the Bible. Our KAIROS impels us *to return to the Bible* and to search the Word of God for a message that is relevant to what we are experiencing in South Africa today. This will be no mere academic exercise. Prophetic theology differs from academic theology in that, whereas academic theology deals with all biblical themes in a systematic manner and formulates general Christian principles and doctrines, prophetic theology concentrates on those aspects of the Word of God that have an immediate bearing upon the critical situation in which we find ourselves. The theology of the prophets does not pretend to be comprehensive and complete, it speaks to the particular circumstances of a particular time and place—the KAIROS.

Consequently a prophetic response and a prophetic theology would include a *reading of the signs of the times.* This is what the great biblical prophets did in their times and this is what Jesus tells us to do. When the Pharisees and Sadducees ask for a sign from heaven, he tells them to "read the signs of the times" (Mt 16:3) or to "interpret this KAIROS" (Lk 12:56). A prophetic theology must try to do this. It must know what is happening, analyse what is happening (social analysis) and then interpret what is happening in the light of the gospel. This means that the starting point for prophetic theology will be our experience of the present KAIROS, our experience of oppression and tyranny, our experience of conflict, crisis and struggle, our experience of trying to be Christians in this situation. It is with this in mind that we must begin to search the scriptures.

Another thing that makes prophetic theology different is that it is always a *call to action.* The prophets do not have a purely theoretical or academic interest in God and in the signs of the times. They call for repentance, conversion and change. They are critical, severely critical, of the status quo; they issue warnings about God's punishment and, in the name of God, they promise great blessings for those who do change. Jesus did the same. "Repent", he says, "the KAIROS has come and the Kingdom of God is close at hand".

Thus prophecy is always *confrontational.* It confronts the evils of the time and speaks out against them in no uncertain terms. Pro-

phetic theology is not afraid to take a stand, clearly and unambigu-
ously. Prophetic statements are stark and simple without being hedged
in with qualifications or possible exceptions. They deal with good
and evil, justice and injustice, God and the devil. It is not surprising
then that any theology that is truly prophetic will be controversial and
in some circles it will be very unpopular. The prophets were persecuted and Jesus was crucified.

Nevertheless, prophetic theology will place a great deal of emphasis upon *hope*. Despite all the criticisms, condemnations and warnings of doom, prophecy always has a message of hope for the future.
After death comes resurrection. That is the prophetic good news.

A genuinely prophetic theology will also be deeply *spiritual*. All
its words and actions will have to be infused with a spirit of fearless-
ness and courage, a spirit of love and understanding, a spirit of joy
and hope, a spirit of strength and determination. A prophetic theology
would have to have in it the mind of Christ, his willingness to suffer
and to die, his humility and his power, his willingness to forgive and
his anger about sin, his spirit of prayer and of action.

Last but not least, prophetic theology should be thoroughly practical and *pastoral*. It will *denounce* sin and *announce* salvation. But
to be prophetic our theology must name the sins and the evils that
surround us and the salvation that we are hoping for. Prophecy must
name the sins of apartheid, injustice, oppression and tyranny in South
Africa today as 'an offence against God' and the measures that must
be taken to overcome these sins and the suffering that they cause. On
the other hand, prophecy will announce the hopeful good news of
future liberation, justice and peace, as God's will and promise, naming
the ways of bringing this about and encouraging people to take action.

4.2 Suffering and Oppression in the Bible[16]

Black Theology, African Theology and the theology of the African
Independent Churches have already laid great emphasis upon the biblical teaching about suffering, especially the suffering of Jesus Christ.

---

16. This section has been rewritten mainly because of the request that more
quotations from the Bible be included in the text.

When we read the Bible from the point of view of our daily experience of suffering and oppression, then what stands out for us is the many, many vivid and concrete descriptions of suffering and oppression throughout the Bible culminating in the cross of Jesus Christ.

For most of their history from Exodus to Revelation, the people of the Bible suffered under one kind of oppression or another: "The sons of Israel are oppressed" (Jer 50:33); "You will be exploited and crushed continually" (Dt 28:33). They were oppressed by the tyrannical, imperial nations around them. First it was the Egyptians: "The Egyptians ill-treated us, they gave us no peace and inflicted harsh slavery upon us" (Dt 26:6). Then the various Canaanite kings oppressed them; for example, Jabin the Canaanite king of Hasor "cruelly oppressed the Israelites for twenty years" (Jud 4:3). And so it carried on with the Philistines, the Assyrians, the Babylonians, the Greeks and the Romans, each in turn exercising an oppressive domination over this small nation.

But this was not all. The people of Israel were also for many centuries oppressed *internally,* within their own country, by the rich and the powerful and especially by the kings or rulers of Israel, who were for the most part typical oriental tyrants. "Here we are now, enslaved; here in the land you gave our Fathers, we are slaves. Its rich fruits swell the profit of the kings who dispose as they please of our bodies and our cattle" (Neh 9:36-37). For the people of South Africa this situation is all too familiar.

The experience of oppression is vividly described in the Bible. First of all, it is described as the painful experience of being crushed to the ground: "Yahweh, they crush your people" (Ps 94:5); "We are bowed in the dust, our bodies crushed to the ground" (Ps 44:25). It is the experience of being weighed down by heavy loads (Ex 1:11; Mt 11:28). But it is more than just an experience of being degraded and humiliated. They lived with the terrifying reality of killings and murders. "We are being massacred daily" (Ps 44:22). "Yahweh, they oppress your hereditary people, murdering and massacring widows, orphans and migrants" (Ps 94:5-6). What grief and torment this causes. "My bones are in torment, my soul is in utter torment. I am worn out with groaning, every night I drench my pillow and soak my bed with tears, my eye is wasted with grief; I have grown old with enemies all round me" (Ps 6:3, 6-10).

Their oppressors were their enemies. The people of Israel were in no doubt about that. There seemed to be no limit to the wickedness and sinfulness of these enemies: greed, arrogance, violence and barbaric cruelty. "My enemies cluster round me, breathing hostility; entrenched in their fat, their mouths utter arrogant claims; now they are closing in. They look like lions eager to tear to pieces" (Ps 17:9-12). "They [the rulers of Israel] have devoured the flesh of my people and torn off their skin and crushed their bones and shredded them like meat" (Mic 3:3).

Only people who had actually experienced oppression could have written such vivid and graphic descriptions of what it means to be oppressed. In South Africa today, in this our KAIROS, more than ever before the people of the townships can identify fully with these descriptions of suffering, oppression and tyranny.

Nor should we think that this concern about oppression is confined to the Old Testament. In the time of Jesus the Jews were oppressed by the Romans, the great imperial superpower of those days. But what was far more immediate and far more pressing was the *internal oppression* of the poor and the ordinary people by the Herods, the rich, the chief priests and elders, the Sadducees and Pharisees. These were the groups who were experienced more immediately as oppressors. In one way or another they were puppets of the Romans and to a greater or lesser extent they collaborated in the oppression of the poor. Jesus calls Herod "that fox" (Lk 13:32). He pronounces "woes" upon the rich (Lk 6:24-26), he calls the Pharisees hypocrites, whited sepulchres and a brood of vipers who lay heavy burdens upon the shoulders of the people and never lift a finger to relieve them (Mt 23 passim). It was the chief priests and the elders who handed Jesus over to the Romans.

Throughout his life Jesus associated himself with the poor and the oppressed, and as the suffering (or oppressed) servant of Yahweh he suffered and died for us. "Ours were the sufferings he bore, ours the sorrows he carried" (Is 53:4). He continues to do so, even today.

4.3 Social Analysis

It is in the light of the biblical teaching about suffering, oppression and tyranny that our prophetic theology must begin to analyse our KAIROS and read the signs of our times. Although it will not be possible to attempt a detailed social analysis or a complete reading of the signs of our times in this document, we must start with at least the broad outlines of an analysis of the conflict in which we find ourselves.

It would be quite wrong to see the present conflict as simply a racial war. The racial component is there, but we are not dealing with two equal races or nations each with its own selfish group interests. The situation we are dealing with here is one of tyranny and oppression. We can therefore use the social categories that the Bible makes use of, namely, *the oppressor and the oppressed.*

What we are dealing with here, in the Bible or in South Africa today, is a social structure. The oppressors are the people who knowingly or unknowingly represent a sinful *cause* and unjust *interests.* The oppressed are people who knowingly or unknowingly represent the opposite *cause* and *interests,* the cause of justice and freedom. Structurally in our society these two causes are in conflict. The individuals involved may or may not realise this, but the structural oppression that in South Africa is called apartheid will sooner or later bring the people involved into conflict.

On the one hand we have the interests of those who benefit from the status quo and who are determined to maintain it at any cost, even at the cost of millions of lives. It is in their interests to introduce a number of reforms in order to ensure that the system is not radically changed and that they can continue to benefit from it as they have done in the past. They benefit from the system because it favours them and enables them to accumulate a great deal of wealth and to maintain an exceptionally high standard of living. And they want to make sure that it stays that way even if some adjustments are needed.

On the other hand we have those who do not benefit in any way from the system the way it is now. They are treated as mere labour units, paid starvation wages, separated from their families by migratory labour, moved about like cattle and dumped in homelands to starve—and all for the benefit of a privileged minority. They have no say in the system and are supposed to be grateful for the concessions that are offered to them like crumbs. It is not in their interests to allow this system to continue even in some 'reformed' or 'revised' form. They are no longer prepared to be crushed, oppressed and exploited. They are determined to change the system radically so that it no longer benefits only the privileged few. And they are willing to do this even at the cost of their own lives. What they want is justice for all irrespective of race, colour, sex or status.

Each of the two sides can be further subdivided according to the different opinions people or groups have about the means and strategies to be used to maintain the system or the means and strategies to be used to change it. An almost infinite variety of opinion is possible here and much debate and discussion is needed, as long as one does not lose sight of the fundamental structural division between efforts to continue oppression even in a mitigated or changed form and efforts to do away with oppression in principle and in every form. There are two conflicting projects here, and no compromise is possible. Either we have full and equal justice for all or we don't.

Prophetic theology therefore faces us with this fundamental choice that admits of no compromises. Jesus did the same. He faced the people with the fundamental choice between God and money. "You cannot serve two masters" (Mt 6:24). Once we have made our choice, once we have taken sides, then we can begin to discuss the morality and effectiveness of means and strategies. It is therefore not primarily a matter of trying to reconcile individual people but a matter of trying to change unjust structures so that people will not be pitted against one another as oppressor and oppressed.

This is our KAIROS. The structural inequality (political, social and economic) expressed in discriminatory laws, institutions and practices has led the people of South Africa into a virtual civil war and rebellion against tyranny.

4.4 Tyranny

According to our Christian tradition, based upon what we have already seen in the Bible, once it is established beyond doubt that a particular ruler is a tyrant or that a particular regime is tyrannical, it forfeits the moral right to govern and the people acquire the right to resist and to find the means to protect their own interests against injustice and oppression. In other words, a tyrannical regime has no *moral legitimacy*. It may be the *de facto* government and it may even be recognised by other governments and therefore be the *de iure* or legal government. But if it is a tyrannical regime, it is, from a moral and a theological point of view, *illegitimate*.

There are indeed some differences of opinion in the Christian tradition about the means that might be used to replace a tyrant, *but* there has not been any doubt about our Christian duty to refuse to cooperate with tyranny and to do whatever we can to remove it.

Of course everything hinges on the definition of a tyrant. At what point does a government become a tyrannical regime?

The traditional Latin definition of a tyrant is *hostis boni communis*—an enemy of the common good. The purpose of all government is the promotion of what is called the common good of the people governed. To promote the common good is to govern in the interests of, and for the benefit of, all the people. Many governments fail to do this at times. There might be this or that injustice done to some of the people. And such lapses would indeed have to be criticised. But occasional acts of injustice would not make a government into an enemy of the people, a tyrant.

To be the enemy of the people a government would have to be hostile to the common good in principle. Such a government would be acting against the interests of the people as a whole and permanently. This would be clearest in cases where the very policy of a government is hostile towards the common good and where the government has a mandate to rule in the interests of some of the people rather than in the interests of all the people. Such a government would be in principle *irreformable*. Any reform that it might try to introduce would not be calculated to serve the common good but to serve the interests of the minority from whom it received its mandate.

A tyrannical regime cannot continue to rule for very long without becoming more and more violent. As the majority of the people begin to demand their rights and to put pressure on the tyrant, so will the tyrant resort more and more to desperate, cruel, gross and ruthless forms of tyranny and repression. The reign of a tyrant always ends up as a reign of terror. It is inevitable because from the start the tyrant is an enemy of the common good.

That leaves us with the question of whether the present government of South Africa is tyrannical or not. There can be no doubt what the majority of the people of South Africa think. For them the regime apartheid is indeed the enemy of the people and that is precisely what they call it: the enemy. In the present crisis, more than ever before, the regime has lost any legitimacy that it might have had in the eyes of the people. Are the people right or wrong?

Apartheid is a system whereby a minority regime elected by one small section of the population is given an explicit mandate to govern in the interests of, and for the benefit of, the white community. Such a mandate or policy is by definition hostile to the common good of all the people. In fact, because it tries to rule in the exclusive interests of whites and not in the interests of all, it ends up ruling in a way that is not even in the interests of those whites. It becomes an enemy of all the people. A tyrant. A totalitarian regime. A reign of terror.

This also means that the apartheid minority regime is irreformable. We cannot expect the apartheid regime to experience a conversion or change of heart and totally abandon the policy of apartheid. It has no mandate from its electorate to do so. Any reforms or adjustments it might make would have to be done in the interests of those who elected it. Individual members of the government could experience a real conversion and repent, but if they did, they would simply have to follow this through by leaving a regime that was elected and put into power precisely because of its policy of apartheid.

And that is why we have reached the present impasse. As the oppressed majority becomes more insistent and puts more and more pressure on the tyrant by means of boycotts, strikes, uprisings, burnings and even armed struggle, the more tyrannical will this regime become. On the one hand it will use repressive measures: detentions, trials, killings, torture, bannings, propaganda, states of emergency and other desperate and tyrannical methods. And on the other hand it will introduce reforms that will always be unacceptable to the majority because all its reforms must ensure that the white minority remains on top.

A regime that is in principle the enemy of the people cannot suddenly begin to rule in the interests of all the people. It can only be replaced by another government—one that has been elected by the majority of the people with an explicit mandate to govern in the interests of all the people.

A regime that has made itself the enemy of the people has thereby also made itself the enemy of God. People are made in the image and likeness of God, and whatever we do to the least of them we do to God (Mt 25:49, 45).

To say that the State or the regime is the enemy of God is not to say that all those who support the system are aware of this. On the whole they simply do not know what they are doing. Many people have been blinded by the regime's propaganda. They are frequently quite ignorant of the consequences of their stance. However, such blindness does not make the State any less tyrannical or any less an enemy of the people and an enemy of God.

On the other hand the fact that the State is tyrannical and an enemy of God is no excuse for hatred. As Christians we are called upon to love our enemies (Mt 5:44). It is not said that we should not or will not have enemies or that we should not identify tyrannical regimes as indeed our enemies. But once we have identified our enemies, we must endeavour to love them. That is not always easy. But then we must also remember that the most loving thing we can do for *both* the oppressed *and* for our enemies who are oppressors is to eliminate the oppression, remove the tyrants from power and establish a just government for the common good of *all the people.*

4.5 Liberation and Hope in the Bible

The Bible, of course, does not only *describe* oppression, tyranny and suffering. The message of the Bible is that oppression is sinful and wicked, an offence against God. The oppressors are godless sinners and the oppressed are suffering because of the sins of their oppressors. But there is *hope* because Yahweh, the God of the Bible, will *liberate* the oppressed from their suffering and misery. "He will redeem their lives from exploitation and outrage" (Ps 74:14). "I have seen the miserable state of my people in Egypt. I have heard their appeal to be free of their slave-drivers. I mean to deliver them out of the hands of the Egyptians" (Ex 3:7).

Throughout the Bible God appears as the liberator of the oppressed: "For the plundered poor, for the needy who groan, now I will act, says Yahweh" (Ps 12:5). God is not neutral. He does not attempt to reconcile Moses and Pharaoh, to reconcile the Hebrew slaves with their Egyptian oppressors or to reconcile the Jewish people with any of their later oppressors. "You have upheld the justice of my cause . . . judging in favour of the orphans and exploited so that earthborn man (human beings) may strike fear no more. My enemies are in retreat, stumbling, perishing as you confront them. Trouble is coming to the rebellious, the defiled, the tyrannical city" (Pss 9:4; 10:18; 9:3; Zeph 3:1). Oppression is a crime, and it cannot be compromised with, it must be done away with. "They [the rulers of Israel] will cry out to God. But he will not answer them. He will hide his face at that time because of all the crimes they have committed" (Mic 3:4). "God, who does what is right, is always on the side of the oppressed" (Ps 103:6).

There can be no doubt that Jesus, the Son of God, also takes up the cause of the poor and the oppressed and identifies himself with their interests. When he stood up in the synagogue at Nazareth to announce his mission he made use of the words of Isaiah.

> The Spirit of the Lord has been given to me.
> For he has anointed me.
> He has sent me to bring the good news to the poor,
> to proclaim liberty to captives
> and to the blind new sight,
> to set the downtrodden free,
> to proclaim the Lord's year of favour. (Lk 4:18-19)

Not that Jesus is unconcerned about the rich and the oppressed. These he calls to repentance. At the very heart of the gospel of Jesus Christ and at the very centre of all true prophecy is a message of hope. Jesus has taught us to speak of this hope as the coming of God's kingdom. We believe that God is at work in our world turning hopeless and evil situations to good so that God's kingdom may come and God's will may be done on earth as it is in heaven. We believe that goodness and justice and love will triumph in the end and that tyranny and oppression cannot last forever. One day "all tears will be wiped away"

(Rev. 7:17; 12:4) and "the lamb will lie down with the lion" (Is 11:6). True peace and true reconciliation are not only desirable, they are assured and guaranteed. This is our faith and our hope. We believe in and hope for the resurrection.

4.6 A Message of Hope

Nothing could be more relevant and more necessary at this moment of crisis in South Africa than the Christian message of hope. As the crisis deepens day by day, what both the oppressor and the oppressed can legitimately demand of the Churches is a message of hope. Most of the oppressed people in South Africa today and especially the youth do have hope. They are acting courageously and fearlessly because they have a sure hope that liberation will come. Often enough their bodies are broken, but nothing can now break their spirit. But hope needs to be confirmed. Hope needs to be maintained and strengthened. Hope needs to be spread. The people need to hear it said again and again that God is with them and that "the hope of the poor is never brought to nothing" (Ps 9:18).

On the other hand the oppressor and those who believe the propaganda of the oppressor are desperately fearful. They must be made aware of the diabolical evils of the present system and they must be called to repentance. "By what right do you crush my people and grind the face of the poor?" (Is 3:15). But they must also be given something to hope for. At present they have false hopes. They hope to maintain the status quo and their special privileges with perhaps some adjustments, and they fear any real alternative. But there is much more than that to hope for and nothing to fear. Can the Christian message of hope not help them in this matter?

A prophetic theology for our times will focus our attention on the future. What kind of future do the oppressed people of South Africa want? What kind of future do the political organisations of the people want? What kind of future does God want? And how, with God's help, are we going to secure that future for ourselves? We must begin to plan the future now, but above all we must heed God's call to action to secure God's future for ourselves in South Africa.

There is hope. There is hope for all of us. But the road to that hope is going to be very hard and very painful. The conflict and the struggle will intensify in the months and years ahead. That is now inevitable—because of the intransigence of the oppressor. But God is with us. We can only learn to become the instruments of his peace even unto death. We must participate in the cross of Christ if we are to have the hope of participating in his resurrection.

Why is it that this powerful message of hope has not been highlighted in 'Church Theology', in the statements and pronouncements of Church leaders? Is it because they have been addressing themselves to the oppressor rather than to the oppressed? Is it because they do not want to encourage the oppressed to be too hopeful for too much?

Now is the time to act—to act hopefully, to act with full confidence and trust in God.

CHAPTER FIVE

Challenge to Action

5.1 God Sides with the Oppressed

To say that the Church must now take sides unequivocally and consistently with the poor and the oppressed is to overlook the fact that the majority of Christians in South Africa have already done so. By far the greater part of the Church in South Africa is poor and oppressed. Of course it cannot be taken for granted that all who are oppressed have taken up their own cause and are struggling for their own liberation. Nor can it be assumed that all oppressed Christians are fully aware of the fact that their cause is God's cause. Nevertheless it remains true that the Church is already on the side of the oppressed because that is where the majority of its members are to be found. This fact needs to be appropriated and confirmed by the Church as a whole.

At the beginning of this document it was pointed out that the present crisis has highlighted the divisions in the Church. We are a divided Church precisely because not all the members of our Churches have taken sides against oppression. In other words, not all Christians have united themselves with God, "who is always on the side of the oppressed" (Ps 103:6). As far as the present crisis is concerned, there is only one way forward to Church unity and that is for those Christians who find themselves on the side of the oppressor, or sitting on the fence, to cross over to the other side to be united in faith and action with those who are oppressed. Unity and reconciliation within the Church itself is only possible around God and Jesus Christ, who are to be found on the side of the poor and the oppressed.

If this is what the Church must become, if this is what the Church as a whole must have as its project, how then are we to translate it into concrete and effective action?

5.2 Participation in the Struggle

Christians, if they are not doing so already, must quite simply participate in the struggle for liberation and for a just society. The campaigns of the people, from consumer boycotts to stayaways, need to be supported and encouraged by the Church. Criticism will sometimes be necessary, but encouragement and support will be necessary as well. In other words, the present crisis challenges the whole Church to move beyond a mere 'ambulance ministry' to a ministry of involvement and participation.[17]

5.3 Transforming Church Activities

The Church has its own specific activities: Sunday services, communion services, baptisms, Sunday school, funerals and so forth. It also has its specific way of expressing its faith and its commitment, that is,

---

17. However, the Church must participate in the struggle as a *Church* and not as a political organisation. Individual Christians as citizens of this country can and must join the political organisations that are struggling for justice and liberation, but the Church as Church must not become a political organisation or subject itself to the dictates of any political party. The Church has its own motivation, its own inspiration for participating in the struggle for justice and peace. The Church has its own beliefs and its own values that impel it to become involved, alongside of other organisations, in God's cause of liberation for the oppressed. The Church will have its own way of operating and it may sometimes have its own special programmes and campaigns, but it does not have, and cannot have, its own political blueprint for the future, its own political policy, because the Church is not a political party. It has another role to play in the world.

The individual Christian, therefore, is both a member of the Church and a member of society, and, on both accounts, Christians should be involved in doing what is right and just. The same is no doubt true of people who adhere to other religious faiths.

in the form of confessions of faith. All of these activities must be reshaped to be more fully consistent with a prophetic faith related to the KAIROS that God is offering us today. The evil forces we speak of in baptism must be named. We know what these evil forces are in South Africa today. The unity and sharing we profess in our communion services or Masses must be named. It is the solidarity of the people inviting all to join in the struggle for God's peace in South Africa. The repentance we preach must be named. It is repentance for our share of the guilt for the suffering and oppression in our country.

Much of what we do in our Church services has lost its relevance to the poor and the oppressed. Our services and sacraments have been appropriated to serve the need of the individual for comfort and security. Now these same Church activities must be reappropriated to serve the real religious needs of all the people and to further the liberating mission of God and the Church in the world.

5.4 Special Campaigns

Over and above its regular activities the Church would need to have special programmes, projects and campaigns because of the special needs of the struggle for liberation in South Africa today. But there is a very important caution here. The Church must avoid becoming a 'Third Force', a force between the oppressor and the oppressed.[18] The Church's programmes and campaigns must not duplicate what the people's organisations are already doing and, even more seriously, the Church must not confuse the issue by having programmes that run counter to the struggles of those political organisations that truly represent the grievances and demands of the people. Consultation, coordination and cooperation will be needed. We all have the same goals even when we differ about the final significance of what we are struggling for.

---

18. There has been a lot of debate about whether the Church should be a "Third Force" or not. It is closely related to the question of whether the Church should take sides or not, which we explained in the previous note. The whole question and the full debate will be dealt with in a forthcoming book entitled *The Kairos Debate*.

5.5 Civil Disobedience

Once it is established that the present regime has no moral legitimacy and is in fact a tyrannical regime certain things follow for the Church and its activities. In the first place *the Church cannot collaborate with tyranny*. It cannot or should not do anything that appears to give legitimacy to a morally illegitimate regime. Second, the Church should not only pray for a change of government, it should also mobilise its members in every parish to begin to think and work and plan for a change of government in South Africa. We must begin to look ahead and begin working now with firm hope and faith for a better future. And finally the moral illegitimacy of the apartheid regime means that the Church will have to be involved at times in *civil disobedience*. A Church that takes its responsibilities seriously in these circumstances will sometimes have to confront and to disobey the State in order to obey God.

5.6 Moral Guidance

The people look to the Church, especially in the midst of our present crisis, for moral guidance. In order to provide this the Church must first make its stand absolutely clear and never tire of explaining and dialoguing about it. It must then help people to understand their rights and their duties. There must be no misunderstanding about the *moral duty* of all who are oppressed to resist oppression and to struggle for liberation and justice. The Church will also find that at times it does need to curb excesses and to appeal to the consciences of those who act thoughtlessly and wildly.

But the Church of Jesus Christ is not called to be a bastion of caution and moderation. The Church should challenge, inspire and motivate people. It has a message of the cross that inspires us to make sacrifices for justice and liberation. It has a message of hope that challenges us to wake up and to act with hope and confidence. The Church must preach this message not only in words and sermons and statements but also through its actions, programmes, campaigns and divine worship services.

CHAPTER SIX

Conclusion

As we said at the beginning, there is nothing final about this document nor even about this second edition. Our hope is that it will continue to stimulate discussion, debate, reflection and prayer, but, above all, that it will lead to action. We invite all committed Christians to take this matter further, to do more research, to develop the themes we have presented here or to criticise them and to return to the Bible, as we have tried to do, with the question raised by the crisis of our times.

Although the document suggests various modes of involvement it does not prescribe the particular actions anyone should take. We call upon all those who are committed to this prophetic form of theology to use the document for discussion in groups, small and big, to determine an appropriate form of action, depending on their particular situation, and to take up the action with other related groups and organisations.

The challenge to renewal and action that we have to set out here is addressed to the Church. But that does not mean that it is intended only for Church leaders. The challenge of the faith and of our present KAIROS is addressed to all who bear the name Christian. None of us can simply sit back and wait to be told what to do by our Church leaders or by anyone else. We must all accept responsibility for acting and living out our Christian faith in these circumstances. We pray that God will help all of us to translate the challenge of our times into action.

We, as theologians (both lay and professional), have been greatly challenged by our own reflections, our exchange of ideas and our discoveries as we met together in smaller and larger groups to prepare this document or to suggest amendments to it. We are convinced that this challenge comes from God and that it is addressed to all of us. We see the present crisis or KAIROS as indeed a divine visitation.

And finally we would also like to repeat our call to our Christian brothers and sisters throughout the world to give us the necessary support in this regard so that the daily loss of so many young lives may be brought to a speedy end.

Study Questions for *The Kairos Document*

(*Note:* a full discussion guide, prepared by David Mesenbring and offering suggestions for five study sessions, is available in Willis H. Logan, ed., *The Kairos Covenant: Standing with South African Christians,* Friendship Press, Meyer-Stone, New York and Oak Park, 1988, pp. 155-78.

Numbers in parentheses below refer to the numbered paragraphs of the text.)

Preface and Introduction

What method was used to create this document? In what kinds of situations would it be useful in our own church life?

Chapter One: The Moment of Truth

1. What is the starting point for reflection in the document?

2. Why is a *kairos* "dangerous" as well as "serious"?

3. What does it mean to say that "The Church is divided against itself"? Are there any analogies to this in the United States?

Chapter Two: Critique of 'State Theology'

1. In what way is Romans 13 a justification for the status quo? *A challenge to it? (2.1)*

2. If "law and order" is the cornerstone of the state, can Christians challenge the state without breaking the law or upsetting the order? (2.2)

3. How real is "the threat of communism" today? Have things changed since the document was written? How relevant is the fear in the United States? (2.3)

4. How different is the South African "God of the State" from the manipulative use made of religion by our own politicians (and occasionally by our preachers as well)? Do they also incur the charge of being "heretical" or "blasphemous"? Do we? (2.4)

Chapter Three: Critique of 'Church Theology'

Four sins of the "English-speaking churches" are analyzed in this chapter. In each case, reflect on their counterparts in the U.S. church.

1. Do we appeal to "reconciliation" as the supreme communal virtue so that we can avoid "conflict" and unpleasant scenes? Is it really possible to "reconcile" good and evil? Why is it "wrong to try to preserve 'peace' and 'unity' at all costs"? Should that not be the goal of every church? (3.1)

2. Why does the "justice of reform" get such rough treatment in the document? If individuals are converted, won't they gradually change the whole society? Why won't "reform from the top" work? (3.2)

3. What is overlooked in conventional Christian appeals to "nonviolence"? Is there a difference between overt physical violence (riots, rocks, burnings, etc.) and the violence of the established structures (that deny employment, withhold food, separate races, prohibit health care to those without money, etc.)? Is there a difference between "violence" and "self-defense"? (3.3)

4. Is "the fundamental problem" in the church found in such things as its "lack of social analysis," its inadequate political strategy, and its individualistic spirituality? Why are these so important to the life of the *church*? Does attention to them reduce the church to being just another social agency? (3.4)

Chapter Four: Towards a Prophetic Theology

1. Seven characteristics of a prophetic theology are cited in this chapter. How can these be reconciled with one another, e.g., being *both* "confrontational" *and* "deeply spiritual"? or "reading the signs of the times" and still having "hope"? (4.1)

2. In the light of the desperate oppression described in the Bible, how can we speak of the power of a loving God? (4.2)

3. If the conflict in South Africa is not "simply a racial war," what is the root of the conflict? Who are the "oppressors" and the "oppressed"? Are such distinctions useful in the United States?

Compare "structural inequality" in South Africa and North America. (4.3)

4. Are there any connections or similarities between the blatant "tyranny" in South Africa and more subtle forms of tyranny in the United States? How does one combine "loving the enemy" with forthright attempts at radical change in order to topple the enemy? (4.4)

5. How can we reconcile the notion that God loves all people with the claim that "God is not neutral," and that God "is always on the side of the oppressed"? How can this be described as a sign of hope for the rest of us? (4.5)

Chapter Five: Challenge to Action

The chapter proposes five courses of specific action to bring about change in South Africa. How could these be adapted to church life in the United States? Are they actually needed in our situation? (5.2–5.6)

Conclusion

The document concludes with a cry for "the necessary support . . . so that the daily loss of so many young lives may be brought to a speedy end." What kinds of specific economic and political policies would be needed in our own national life if we were to take this cry seriously?

Kairos Central America

A Challenge to the
Churches of the World

Introduction

Clearly stimulated by the publication of the South African *kairos* document and the extraordinary response to it, a group of Christian leaders in Central America gathered to discuss the possibility of issuing a similar document addressed to their own situation. Following the same pattern of reflection-action-reflection-action, a variety of groups in the various countries of Central America created the document reprinted below, issued on April 3, 1988, with more than a hundred signers out of many hundreds who had shared in the process of its creation. The signers were drawn from a wide variety of denominations and backgrounds, including laypeople, members of religious orders, Protestant pastors, Catholic priests, and even three bishops. A few North Americans living and working in Central America also signed the document. Because the text contains "controversial" material, the names of most of the participants from El Salvador, Guatemala, and Honduras were omitted from the list, since a record of participation would have made them highly vulnerable back home. The other countries represented by the signatories were Nicaragua, Costa Rica, Panama, Mexico, and Belize.

As in the case of the South African counterpart, the writers consider their document "open-ended" and invite readers to send comments, suggestions, and reflections to *Kairos Central America* Document, Apartado 3205 (or Apartado RP-082), Managua, Nicaragua.

Kairos Central America

A Challenge to the Churches
of the World

Contents

Introduction

1. This document is addressed to all those Christians and persons of goodwill who have followed our people's situation and struggles, and who pray and act in solidarity with us in all the countries of the world.
2. Through this document we want to encourage them to continue in solidarity with our struggle and our hope. We need the Christians of the entire world to stay firm and constant in their solidarity with Central America.
3. We address ourselves with special urgency to Christian communities in our own Central America and in the United States, since they are the peoples most directly involved in the conflicts that our region is going through.
4. As we share our testimony of faith with you, we want also to appeal to our own consciences as Central American Christians. We feel and believe that we are arriving at a moment for uniting more closely and for coming to common decisions. We must watch and pray, ponder and try to discern the signs of the times. Only in that way will we be able to make choices and carry out actions that are in keeping with the desires and cries of our people. As Christians we have the obligation to contribute towards achieving a worthwhile peace that is the result of defending and respecting our free self-determination and of working toward justice and brotherhood and sisterhood.
5. Central American "Kairos" arises from 464 years of struggle,

agony and hope. The confrontation with the United States' neo-colonial and interventionist policy is coming to a head in the entire region. The war of aggression against Nicaragua; the constant pressure put on the Central American governments, including those of Belize and Panama, by the United States government to support its policies; the occupation of Honduras as a military staging ground and the military support for the repressive regimes of Guatemala and El Salvador all endanger the lives of the region's more than 22 million human beings. Our peoples, already impoverished by unjust national and international economic systems, groan and struggle in courage and hope.

6. We humbly admit that we have not arrived at a full and satisfactory understanding of this difficult hour. Nevertheless, in spite of our limitations, we want to contribute this first word, to put in motion a process of shared analysis, reflection and insight that will continue to spread more light each day for all of us here in Central America, as well as at an international level.

7. We do not intend to give the last word with this *Kairos Central America* document. Rather, our desire is to share our faith and our Christian reading of this historical hour we are living out in Central America in humility, and in this way create an opening for reflection and dialog in communities and churches, together with all persons of goodwill. We invite all the communities to pray, reflect, discern and formulate their own Christian view of this Kairos that is Central America, and to share that understanding with other communities in a prophetic exercise of shared solidarity and Christian coresponsibility in this hour of Central America's history.

8. We invite you to distribute this our document, and we cheerfully urge you to send your reactions, suggestions, reflections and criticisms, or, even better, your own *Kairos Central America* document to: Apartado 3205 or Apartado RP-082 in Managua, Nicaragua.

Thank You.

PART I

The Reality We Live In

***

9. *1) Life in Central America*
During the last ten years more than 200,000 persons out of a total of 25 million inhabitants of the region (about 1%) have died (violently) in Central America. In large part, these were poor people: labor union members, Indians, peasants, guerrilla fighters, cooperative members and young people forcefully recruited to fight against their own brothers and sisters. All were victims of a policy of terror and counter-insurgency.

10. This war is not an accident, nor is it the result of the Central American's violent nature. It is the product of injustice. It is the struggle of the poor majorities in defense of their lives, against the privileged groups that have always kept economic, political and military power for themselves. These groups have continually received financing and support from United States governments that defends its presence and influence at the cost of Third World nations.

11. The armed conflicts in our countries are nothing else than dramatic expressions of institutionalized violence. In Nicaragua the counterrevolutionaries, armed and financed by the U.S. government, have committed thousands of assassinations among the civilian population, just as in El Salvador and Guatemala where the government's armies play this genocidal role.

12. The economic war against the majorities is one expression of this institutionalized violence. Among its victims we can mention:

13. Those who in the cities and countryside organize themselves in labor unions and other democratic associations to defend their lives, and who are victims of repression, disappearances, torture and death.

14. Women who are forced to migrate to the cities and offer themselves as domestic servants or prostitutes.

15. Workers who see their real income constantly diminishing. A large number of unemployed and underemployed. Massive migration toward countries to the North, in search of employment and security.

16. Hundreds of thousands of peasants displaced from their traditional homes because military operations make it impossible for them to cultivate their lands.

17. Miners and timber workers exploited by transnational corporations which destroy the environment.

18. Emigration of technical workers in search of jobs.

19. Divided families, orphaned children, single mothers.

20. The high percentage of illiteracy in the major part of the region is another form of institutionalized violence. Cultural invasion that presents the North American way of life as paradise. Insufficient health delivery services, along with high levels of infant mortality.

21. The war has common roots, but it finds a different expression in each country. In *Nicaragua,* a young revolutionary state struggles to defend what it has achieved, its sovereignty and independence, against a North American administration that has declared war at all levels: diplomatic, economic, political, social and military making use of counter-revolutionary bands. In *Guatemala,* the traditional dictatorship takes the form of a Christian Democrat government, a disguise for the genocide and ethnocide that are flaring up again. In *El Salvador* the people's guerrilla movement is growing, offering an alternative to the puppet government backed by the U.S. In *Honduras* the real power is in the hands of the military who represent the aggressive, militaristic policy of the United States. In *Costa Rica* a democracy is being weakened and losing credibility, due to impoverishment and debt. In *Panama* a long and difficult nationalist struggle culminated in the signing of the Torrijos-Carter treaties (1977) which promise to return the interoceanic canal, their principal resource, to the

Panamanians. Empire seeks to break these agreements in a thousand different ways.

22. *2) Antecedents*
Central America's present struggle begins with the conquest of our peoples under Spain's colonialist policy in the sixteenth century, the pillaging of their natural resources and the exploitation of the natives under the "legitimacy" of the Spanish crown, the cross and the sword. The indigenous population was submitted to a regime of slave labor in agriculture and mining. There were centuries of lopsided struggle by Spaniards and Creoles against Indians and black slaves brought from Africa, of expropriating their lands, their culture and their lives. A few nations, such as the Mayas and Caribs, managed a certain degree of independence. These peoples are still struggling to survive.

23. Independence from Spain, resulting from her political and economic deterioration, did nothing to better the conditions of our countries' inhabitants. The privileged minorities retained their advantageous position within this new phenomenon. The nineteenth century witnessed a constant fight between Conservatives and Liberals. It was only in the second half of the century that Central America became incorporated into the capitalist system of production via agro-export economies built principally of coffee. This meant an even greater plundering of the impoverished masses, with the peasants being converted into day workers on the coffee and banana plantations.

24. The history of our tiny republics, divided up during the first half of the nineteenth century by the interests of the classes in power, is the story of their search for a political and economic model to follow. Nicaragua saw its sovereignty attacked by North American interests related to an interoceanic route. Nicaragua was also the scene of Central America's just war against the filibuster Walker, as well as of the army for the Defense of Sovereignty led by Cesar Augusto Sandino against the U.S. Army's invasion in 1927. There have been similar interests of the North Americans related to the Panama Canal. Here a nationalist campaign resulted in the Torrijos-Carter accords for the return of the Canal. Numberless maneuvers by the U.S. to break them have created the present conflicts.

25. In Guatemala, in 1954 a military coup set up by the CIA, which put together a mercenary army in Honduras, destroyed a democratic, popular participative government that had been attained for the first time.

26. Military regimes have struck the dominant note in our nations, and have meant antipopular and repressive dictatorships. A clear example of this was the massacre in El Salvador in 1932 of 30,000 peasants who had risen up against hunger and the lack of democracy. Costa Rica remained a civilian island within this tendency. Regional military alliances (CONDECA) were nothing but counterrevolutionary policies, reflected most clearly in the National Security Doctrine adopted to "prevent" any attempt to set up a new Cuba in the region, Cuba being a people who had shown the road toward building a new society.

27. At the present, militarism continues to be the spinal column of U.S. policy for dominating the area. Its military bases in Panama and Honduras confirm this.

28. Expressions of public resistance have not been absent during any period. In recent years the FSLN achieved, together with the people, Nicaragua's liberation. In both El Salvador and Guatemala, peoples' political-military organizations represent a viable alternative.

29. *3) Geopolitical Presence in Central America*
The Central American peoples' struggle has global implications. Today there are urgent demands for a new international order in the economic, political and juridical fields. The attempt is to replace the right of power by the power of right in international relations.

30. The moral force of this geopolitical position rests on its popular support in Central America. The popular Sandinista Revolution is a building in Nicaragua, and in its new constitution an original plan for complete democracy has been set into place; a democracy that is participative (through its mass organizations: youth, women, workers, etc.) and representative (pluralism of political parties that take part in the Legislative Assemblies). An important element of this popular and participative democracy is the creation and protection of the opportunity for cultural and political autonomy on the part of ethnic groups. Without this kind of participation by the indigenous communities there can be no true democracy in the countries of the area.

31. It is no accident that the Central American peoples' struggles have served as the occasion for organizing an active block of Latin

American nations. First the Contadora Group organized, made up of Mexico, Venezuela, Colombia and Panama, to seek a negotiated solution to the Central American conflicts as an alternative to the military and anti-people solutions promoted by the U.S. Later on Brazil, Argentina, Peru and Uruguay joined the group. In this way Central America has served to pull together the "Bolivar countries", a fact which is changing the relationship between the United States and Latin America. Even the Organization of American States (OAS), formerly an instrument of U.S. interests, has achieved a certain autonomy. The Latin American nations have taken up the self-determination and nonintervention banners, causes which in former times were nothing more than the expression of helpless countries' desires, but which today are transformed by their unity into a political platform that is respected among the concert of the nations as a Latin American proposal for a new international political order.

32. The U.S. government, obstinate in its policy of aggression against these small nations that it has always considered as its "backyard", has kept on promoting the counterrevolution, against international law, and against Latin America's desire to seek reasoned solutions.

33. The interpretation of "democracy" and the "democratic governments" that result where "Western" models as designed by the U.S. actually come into being, collide altogether with the feeling and thinking of our peoples. For them (the U.S.), Nicaragua's emerging democracy is totalitarianism and a government that destroys Western values; while regimes like the Christian Democrats in El Salvador and Guatemala that violate human rights and faithfully carry out counterrevolutionary plans are the living images of democracy for them. The Honduras government, militarized and utilized as a base for aggression, is for them a democratic regime that has to be saved from Sandinista expansion threats. We have before us an interpretation of the world that is diametrically opposite.

34. The Esquipulas Agreements process shows our peoples' desire to find a Central American solution for Central American problems. This possibility of a negotiated settlement, without outside interference, is constantly being threatened by U.S. intransigence when confronted with fair solutions.

35. *4) Christians in Central America*

The most important new feature of church life within the peoples' struggle in Central America is the participation by sizable Christian groups in these peoples' movements and in the peoples' armed forces. Beginning with the early ecclesial communities in Olancho (Honduras) and San Miguelito (Panama) up until the incorporation of individual Christians and some communities in Nicaragua's insurrection, including Indian and non-Indian communities in Guatemala, there are Christians who are immersed in this experience, and even form a specific sector of the revolutionary struggles.

36. As a result of this Christian militancy, the number of Central American martyrs has multiplied—Christians who have been assassinated for following Jesus. The martyrdom of Oscar Arnulfo Romero, the Archbishop of San Salvador, is known by all. Many Delegates of the Word and pastoral workers have been assassinated by the counterrevolution in Nicaragua and by the repressive governments of Guatemala, El Salvador and Honduras because of this testimony to the Word. There are also Christians who have died in combat, after taking up arms for the peoples' cause, motivated by their faith, such as Arlen Siu, Sergio Guerrero Sosa, Father Gaspar Garcia Laviana in Nicaragua, Father Ernesto Barrera in El Salvador, Father Guadalupe in Honduras, etc.

37. There are many testimonies of living faith, both personal and collective: the hope against all hope lived out in the midst of bombing and indiscriminate military operations in Guatemala's mountains and in the resistance communities; communities in zones controlled by the guerrilla in El Salvador, where a "pastoral practice of accompaniment" has developed; communities in Nicaragua's war zones that defend their lives and their work with their arms and their faith.

38. In these last years Central America is furnishing new forms of evangelism. A firing-line pastoral attention immersed in the armed conflict, with the peoples' movements, with the peace movements, all under the Lord's commission to be leaven in the dough. Christians and revolutionaries have begun to dialog and develop common practice, in a new way of relating, not without tensions but full of contributions toward the liberation process.

39. Church authorities have shown a positive attitude in offering their evangelical good offices for humanizing the conflict and mediating in the search for negotiated solutions.

40. All of this participation has led to a new period of theological reflection and pastoring, and an effort to systematize the same and offer it as testimony to churches outside the region. A new kind of spirituality flourishes, a new kind of Christian behaviour that attracts solidarity in a way that has brought new life to many churches in many different countries.

PART II

Seeing This Historic Hour in Central America from a Perspective of Faith

41. We want to plumb the Christian meaning that this historic Central American hour that we are living in has for us. For that we make use of our Christian faith. We feel ourselves enlightened by:

42. a) The words and deeds of Jesus who, living in a critical and conflictive social situation like ours—that of *Pax Romana,* offered and imposed by the Empire—witnessed to the way that leads to true peace, making an unmistakable option for the poor;

43. b) The God who has revealed that God is the God of life and peace, without confusing that with any idolatrous image of God;

44. c) The utopia of the Kingdom, revealed by Jesus as God's will for history and commended by Him to His followers as the most important cause and the supreme object of our action in history.

1. Signs of the Kingdom in This Historic Hour in Central America

Aided by our faith we discover these signs of the Kingdom in Central America:

45. *1.1. The People Become Subjects of History*

We sense that in this hour the historical consciousness of our Central

American peoples is getting to be more mature. The majorities, oppressed for centuries, are becoming aware of their own dignity. They are leaving off being "the masses" to become more and more consciously "the people". The poor break into history as peoples who become the subjects of their own liberation processes.

46. At one and the same time oppressed and believers, this "people that was not a people" is becoming more and more the "people of God". The Spirit has shaken them and has led them to rise up against an oppressive system. In their faith they have found new lights for unmasking injustice and for following Jesus as the one who takes away the world's sin, the liberator from all oppression, the One who gives peace in a different way than the world gives it.

47. From the perspective of faith, we see our people as collective "Servants of Yahweh" elected and called to actively redeem the world by their fruitful sufferings, and establish justice among the nations.

48. Together with Mary of Nazareth, we also proclaim the greatness of God, because God sees the humiliation of God's poor, pulls down the mighty from their thrones and fights at our side to deliver us from the hand of our enemies. Something of the Kingdom's utopia comes into being historically when the poor peoples' peace project advances, when obstacles that keep them from living with dignity are removed. There is something of the divine in the struggle for the rights of the poor, which are also God's rights. We feel the greatness and glory of God when the poor have access to abundant life and peace, when they struggle together as a people to build the Kingdom in history.

49. The fact that the poor people, God's people, become subjects of history is a piece of Good News that only the little ones and those who look from their point of view are capable of comprehending. Only to them has it been given to understand these things, to discover this sign of the Kingdom which is "joy for all the people" (Lk. 2:10-12).

50. *1.2. The People's Peace Project Advances*
Our soil is rich and fertile, but through the centuries the successive empires have pillaged our wealth, in league with the compliant local oligarchies and enjoying the church's blessing. Thus they have robbed us of the very elements of our life: food, health, education, land,

housing and work. For this reason there is no peace. For this reason there is war in Central America.

51. Our peoples have said "Enough!" They are rising up on their feet, they are uniting in rebellion, they are attempting to arrive at peace based on the peoples' rights (without placing their hope in the powerful), within Central American and Latin American unity, going beyond the forms and institutions that only serve the Empire, sustained by international help and solidarity.

52. In these small steps that peace is taking toward us, small steps if we take into account the magnitude of the task that awaits us still, we see the Kingdom of God that is Peace, Justice and Life for the poor draw near.

53. *1.3. The Cross and the Persecution of the Kingdom*
Just as yesterday, Jesus and His cause are signs of contradiction today. In this His disciples are not less than our Master. Today, as yesterday, the powerful insist on perpetuating the oppressive system. They keep on imposing the cross and death on those who dare to struggle for the same cause as Jesus. They want to keep His Kingdom from coming. They want to prevent the oppressed majorities from becoming peoples, the peoples from becoming church, God's people from becoming a real historical people, the church from becoming incarnate in the people.

54. We see that the persecution, cross and death that the Empire and its accomplices unleash against the people and their peace project, against the rebel poor, against the builders of the Kingdom, is growing fiercer. But, alongside this, this cross and this death, we have seen flourish the testimony of the blood of so many men and women who have laid down and continue to lay down their lives heroically for the cause, for peace, for Jesus' cause. This heritage of martyrdom challenges us, calls us to be faithful, to sacrifice, to heroism, to radical following. This is one of the most precious signs of the Kingdom that comes to us.

55. *1.4. Central America: Prophecy within History by the God of the Poor*
In the process of maturing in their historical consciousness with the help of their faith, Central America's poor came to find out that the

God of Western Christian Society was not the God of Jesus, but rather
an idol of the Empire. They realized that God does not want the
present system (even if it is blessed by institutional churches), but a
new order that implies the destruction of the old.

56. Based on their faith they rose up, and are still rising up against
the old society called "Christian"; they rose up against that God that
was supposedly Christian. But they did not do it in the name of
atheism or against religion. Rather, they appealed explicitly to that
God who is truly Christian, the God whom Jesus rediscovered as
unmistakably the God of the poor and of Life. They keep on in that
struggle, including there where, with the old order destroyed, they
now face Empire's war to impede the establishment and consolidation
of the people's peace project.

57. In that way the war in Central America is a religious and theological war, a struggle between gods that are situated on both sides
of the conflict. The God of the Poor, revealed by Jesus, has once more
heard their cry and has made Himself present to lead the oppressed
to liberation against the oppressors and against their gods.

58. By their rebellion and struggle, by their blood poured out and
their collective martyrdom, they are denouncing as "non-Christian"
the God who justified the conquest and lent itself for blessing successive empires, the very God whom so many Christians of today
keep on invoking while they bless and support the imperial system
itself.

59. The death project that is directed against these oppressed and
believing Central American majorities to overcome their holy rebellion is the most recent edition of the executions and deaths inflicted
"in the name of God and Western Christian civilization" throughout
history.

60. The Central American poor at this time are serving as witnesses
and martyrs for the God of Jesus, the God of the poor. They are a
living prophecy, proclaimed from within a way of life in history, that
invites the Christian churches to abandon Empire's gods and become
converted to the true God, manifested in Jesus, without getting bogged
down in serving two masters.

61. *1.5. The Presence of Salvation in the Liberation Process*
Our peoples are living out a liberation process. We see our struggle

as our last resort, as our only way out for survival, for retaining our dignity in history, as children of God, for collaborating with God in His design for salvation. The Central America war is a war of liberation: we are defending our right to peace against a centuries-old aggression. What is absurd in all this violence above all else is the insistence by the powerful upon keeping the peoples from being free.

62. Faith tells us that the history of God incarnate takes place within human history, that salvation history is the history of our total liberation. For that reason, even while we must distinguish carefully between temporal progress and growth in God's Kingdom, nevertheless temporal progress and progress in the liberation process as well are of great interest for the Kingdom of God. Just as Israel in being liberated from her oppression in Egypt, so we cannot but feel the Lord's saving footsteps present when we arrive at more human living conditions, when peace and life come out to meet us, when we take a step—however small—toward full liberation.

63. While we do not make historical liberation identical with eschatological salvation, we also do not separate them unduly. We neither separate them nor confuse them. There is a presence of the Kingdom-mysterious, the object of faith—where the peoples' liberation process advances, even though this process may enjoy its own autonomy and methodology. All the outpouring of our peoples' hope and generosity is not something that can be lost in death's abyss. Rather, it is written in the Book of Life with letters of blood, and is part of the definitive Kingdom which is growing mysteriously at present and triumphing day by day in our history, on its way to its final plenitude.

2. Signs of the Anti-Kingdom in This, Central America's Historic Hour

64. *2.1. The Sin against the Holy Spirit*

We acknowledge with joy the Spirit's action in the signs of the Kingdom that occur in our history via the poor, in favor of our peoples' cause, in favor of life and of that peace that is the fruit of justice, in our peoples' liberation processes. . . . All these are the signs that validated, and validate, the messianic function (Lk. 7:18ff.) of Him who came that we might have life and life in abundance (Jn. 10:10). For that reason we believe that as Jesus denounced it (Mk. 3:28ff.), today as yesterday, the sin against the Holy Spirit consists in not recognizing the work and glory of God in all that favors human life, the life of the poor, the peoples' peace.

65. Thus the theology and pastoral practice that continue the theological tradition of legitimizing the conquest and genocide, the domination and oppression, seem to us to be truly sins against the Holy Spirit. Today as well they legitimize the violation of our peoples' sovereignty, the monopolistic transnational capitalism that exploits us, the imperialism that oppresses us, the puppet governments and democratic facades that hide our real condition from the world. . . . This theology and pastoral practice ignore and silence the misery in which our oppressed majorities live and the death that is imposed upon the "prohibited" peoples. The Empire itself supports, promotes, finances and adapts this theology as a deadly weapon against the poor, against their liberation processes, against their liberated Christian faith, and especially against the God of the poor. It is scandalous for our faith that there are Christians and church authorities who commit this sin against the Holy Spirit, in confabulation with the shadowy powers of this sinful world.

66. The fundamentalist apocalyptic theology so present in institutional churches, and above all in the sects, and which asserts that all human work in history is the devil's work until Christ comes, deserves our identical condemnation. Another series of theologies, for their part, consider themselves to be above politics, or sponsor a supposed apoliticism as a line of Christian ethical behaviour. In reality all these theologies represent a false and evasive spiritualism that alienates people, sidetracks them from their responsibilities in history and plays the game of the enemies of the poor by letting itself be used to "satanize" every attempt at liberation, using an irrational anticommunism for the purpose.

67. Accomplices in this sin against the Holy Spirit are so many brothers and sisters, among us and in the First World, whether confessing Christians or not, who remain entrenched in their comforts, using as an excuse the distance, the lack of clear information, the varying interpretations, the complexity of the problems . . . while the poor continue to die and new and larger quotas of blood are imposed on the project of peace and life.

68. *2.2. Sin in the Peoples' Movements*
From the perspective of our faith we see that peoples' movements necessarily are the means by which we serve the Kingdom. That same faith and our commitment at a practical level provide us with the critical insight that we must not place obstacles in the way of what is only a means. As a means, peoples' movements are a human reality that is not exempt from limitations nor free from sin. Our fight against sin is also directed against whatever sin there might be in the means that we use in our struggle on behalf of the Kingdom.

69. For that reason, always with a constructive spirit (constructing the Kingdom), and without losing sight of our final purpose, we feel compelled to contribute our criticisms of, or even to denounce, whatever betrayal, rivalries and even serious internal rifts there are that are put above the peoples' cause and interest, such as withdrawing from the people, or whatever there might be of popularism, militarism, bureaucratism, abuses, discrimination, revenge, inconsistency or infidelity in the peoples' movements.

70. In the same way we ask God's forgiveness and that of our brothers and sisters in a spirit of self-criticism and repentance, feeling ourselves to be sinners who are called continually to conversion, for all that there is of sin and scandal in our personal and collective lives—personal inconsistencies, weariness and faint-heartedness, community conflicts, anti-evangelical attitudes, ambition for power or desires to rule, intolerance and suspicion, lack of generosity in our pardoning, cowardliness in the face of the radical demands placed on us by the defense of the rights of the poor. . . . We are in constant search of the New Human Being that we long to arrive at.

71. Our criticism and self-criticism, firm and sincere at the same time that it is constructive and faithful, makes up a part of the positive contribution that we from our faith feel obliged to give unconditionally to the cause of our peoples' liberation. Jesus, who so clearly supported His people's cause, did not hesitate to "challenge" His people when loyalty to the higher cause of the Kingdom demanded it.

72. *2.3. Manipulating the Defense of "Democracy" and "Human Rights"*

Democracy and human rights are for us a step forward in human history, a conquest that must not be surrendered and that has to be constantly strengthened. Therefore, we cannot join in with those who want to give them a restrictive meaning, nor with those who manipulate this people's cause against the very interests of the people. For example:

73. When this is used to hide repressive and genocidal regimes that are guilty of tens of thousands of disappearances and assassinations behind a facade of electoral democracy—regimes that rob the people of the fundamental things of life in favor of the luxury and privileges of a scandalously tiny minority;

74. When it is used to support secretly the plans of a political party like the Christian Democrats that act as a legitimizing force for systems of domination;

75. When it is used to avoid facing up to a universal questioning of the present world order, the imperial order, the system that gives privilege to the powerful, the "Western Christian Civilization".

76. Proclaiming a formal electoral democracy, or civil and political rights in their liberal bourgeois sense is not enough. Stopping at that point, or utilizing that proclamation to combat the possibility of a true "people's government", or to ignore or even impede that exercise of human rights that works in favor of the peoples as nations, as ethnic groups or as a class in securing their right to sovereignty, self-determination and life for the poor majorities, represents manipulation and a sin against life and against the truth.

77. *2.4. Condemnations of Violence That Themselves Violate Life*
After centuries of tolerating and legitimizing domination through institutionalized violence, glorious prophetic exceptions to the contrary notwithstanding, it was only when the poor opted for defending themselves that the churches finally came out as condemning "all violence, wherever it may come from." The uncritical use of this condemnation, maintained at times through voluntary blindness, equates under the same label the struggle by the poor to defend themselves and survive, and the systematic oppression by the power-

ful, the repression with which they react to the poor when they are not submissive.

78. On the other hand, many church institutions wash the conscience of the privileged oligarchies who are responsible for the institution-alized violence practiced against Central America's majorities, which they legitimize ideologically and bless juridically and ecclesiastically. They place chaplains (priests, pastors and even bishops) at the service of the armies and repressive bodies, or they judge that such violence is necessary for defending "the established order".

79. In this regard it is significant and especially scandalous that Nicaragua, the only country of our region in which the people's project is in power, should be the only place where the majority of the institutional churches and their hierarchies have not condemned "all violence, no matter where it comes from", and have not con-demned the violence practiced by the anti-people forces that Empire maintains.

80. *2.5. Calls for Reconciliation That Sidestep Sin in Central America*

In Central America we frequently hear calls to reconciliation made by the churches who seem to place themselves above the parties in the Central American conflict, appealing to love and to Christian brotherhood and sisterhood. Such calls seem at first glance to be very Christian, but if we seek to come to a careful spiritual understanding, we find that they are not so much so.

81. The Central American conflict is played out between an oppres-sor that is violent and heavily armed and the majorities that have been oppressed, massacred and helpless for centuries. It is a conflict that can only be described in terms of a struggle between justice and injustice, between good and evil, between life and death. In this context the idea of reconciling good with evil not only represents a misapplication of the Christian idea of reconciliation, it is also a twisting of the Christian faith. Our duty is to put an end to evil, to injustice, to oppression and to sin; not to come to an agreement with them. We must not reconcile good with evil, life with death. All Christian reconciliation implies a radical option for justice and for the poor.

82. The peace that the world offers is a "reconciliation" that covers up injustice and oppression. Real peace is the outcome of justice, not the result of arrangements negotiated with injustice. In Central America, as in all of Latin America, there is no other possibility for Christian reconciliation than setting in motion the peoples' peace plan, the plan of the organized and conscious poor, as the opposing alternative to what those who were and are their oppressors have in mind.

83. From the perspective of the Christian faith, we cannot make a call to reconciliation as though it were an order coming from the outside, avoiding our responsibility for the conflict. We definitely have to work for real reconciliation, a reconciliation that we believe possible because we know the people's capacity for pardon as an act of dignity and humanity toward the enemy, once the causes that brought about the injustice and conflict have disappeared.

3. Central America Is a Kairos

84. The analysis we have made and the understanding we have arrived at of the signs and anti-signs of the Kingdom, in the midst of the signs of the times and in the place where we live in Central America, lead us to conclude that this, Central America's historic hour, is a Kairos—a chance for Grace, a decisive hour, an especially tense time within the reaches of salvation history.

85. The Central American crisis has gotten more serious and more profound. The conflict has reached a climax in tension and in deepening of consciousness. Never before in our history have the poor felt themselves so moved by the Wind of the Spirit to be effective instruments for the purposes of the God who is Creator of all. Never before have the churches of Central America felt themselves so engaged and challenged by the God of the poor. Never before has the Empire had to turn so irrationally to "might makes right". Never before has the world had such a generalized feeling of international solidarity and shared responsibility in the face of what is in play in Central America, in the face of what this land is giving birth to for the sake of a New Humanity and a new world.

86. This is the moment. The hour is decisive. It is the passing of God through our history, through Central America. Abel's blood cries out to heaven. Lazarus's shout demands immediate attention. The Central American peoples force their way into the world consciousness as the true judges of our acclaimed brotherhood and sisterhood. The Third World's oppressed masses look to Central America with anxiety and hope. Central America has become a Kairos of unforeseeable consequences: either we close the door on the possibility of hope for the poor for many years, or as prophets we open up a new Day for humanity and thus for the church.

87. This is the Central American Kairos: a chance for grace in which the Lord calls us to take up the challenges of this historic hour. A chance for grace to create a new international order where right makes might and not vice-versa, where peoples who have been denied and humiliated through the centuries become free human beings, to live in sovereignty and self-determination, where small nations can live together in brotherhood and sisterhood without any Empire threatening them. An opportunity for penitently putting right the historical errors of conquest and genocide, to assure a new attitude before the fact of 500 years. An opportunity to amend the churches' sins in our history, to give our commitment and our spirituality a historical footing, to live out our faith in a way that is incarnate in history. A one-time-only opportunity for honoring the blood of so many heroes and martyrs in our history with due reverence; for consoling so many brothers and sisters wounded by pain and death; for transmitting hope and courage to the poor of the earth, so many of whom see in Central America their Older Brother. An opportunity for the grace of conversion by which the First World and the so-called "Western Christian Society" turn to the true Christian God whom the poor permit them to rediscover through their prophetic testimony.

88. This historic hour in Central America is a Kairos, the passing of God incarnate in Jesus, through the burning "waste" of Latin America, calling on us to fight for the Kingdom, to the cross, to unwavering hope, to invincible unity, to resurrection triumph.

4. Our Response to This Central American Kairos

89. *4.1. The Option for the Poor*
It is impossible for us to be Christians in Central America without

taking a position in support of those who are unjustly pushed aside, in support of the oppressed masses, and against the system of death that dominates the world. Only then can we follow Jesus.

90. This historic hour in Central America constitutes a radical call for clear geopolitical definition: you are on the side of the people or you become an accomplice of their oppressors; you are on the side of the poor or you are with the Empire; with the God of Life or with the idols of death; with the God of Jesus or with the false "Christian" god.

91. The Central American Kairos means recognizing the poor peoples' dignity, recognizing their right to be protagonists in their own liberation, to be protagonists of a project of liberation for everybody, but especially for the most oppressed: women, Indian, Afro-Americans. . . .

92. *4.2. Nourishing the Peoples' Hope*

The spiritual experience of God in people in Central America—their faith, their hope, their revolutionary love—nourishes us all. We are witnesses to their martyrs' testimony. And at the same time, we feel ourselves called to add our grain of sand toward nourishing, strengthening and sustaining *their* hope.

93. We want to nourish this vision of faith that leads us to discover the presence of God walking at the head of our peoples, awakening our desires to be free, pushing us along liberation paths, defending us from our oppressors, supplying us with what we need amid the desert's scarcity while we escape beyond Empire's reach.

94. This nourishing of our people's hope will be our best contribution—what is most appropriately and specifically ours as Christians, as leaven in the dough—to the process of our people's liberation, the working out in history of God's liberation plan, the building of the Kingdom in history.

95. *4.3. Being Radical in Our Service to the Kingdom*

In this hour in which we in Central America are living out a historic conflict in which we are torn dramatically between life and death, we cannot but fix our attention on what is most essential in our being Christians and concentrate avidly on God's ultimate purpose in history: God's Kingdom! We want to be radical in our following Jesus, to live and struggle for His cause.

96. We want to avoid the classic temptation that our churches have fallen into for centuries, to think of themselves as their own end and aim, spending their energies on their own inner church life while paying no attention at all to the struggle in history where the coming of the Kingdom and the glory of God is at stake: and even arriving at the conclusion that the business of building the Kingdom in history is a "profane" or "political" activity that is none of their concern.

97. With our eyes fixed on the Kingdom (Jesus' Cause, the absolute around which all mediating activities must be ordered), we want to help our churches to overcome all dichotomies and reductionisms, to become incarnate in the people, to accept the people's prophetic and priestly roles, to abandon their supposed neutrality and overcome their internal divisions while taking an unequivocal stand for the poor. Thus they will get down into the arena of history where under the sign of hope their faith and love can become realities; where they will put at risk their prestige and even their peace; where they will take on persecution and even death itself and with their actions cry out from this land of volcanoes, "Your Kingdom come!" Your will be done on earth, in Central America, as it is in Heaven!

5. Challenges Posed for Our Brothers and Sisters by Central America's Kairos

98. Central America is a Kairos of grace not only for us who live here. We are convinced that it presents a challenge to the churches and the world. Brothers and sisters, permit us to open our hearts humbly and in confidence make some suggestions that can help you receive this Central American Kairos.

99. *We Are Your Neighbors*
We want to give you our answer to that question that perhaps you, like the Scribe in the Gospel, have been asking, "Who is my neighbor?" (Lk. 10:25ff.). We are that "certain man" in Jesus' parable for whom you must be good Samaritans. We are wounded by the roadside, enslaved without pity by successive empires, exploited by the transnationals, repressed and massacred by military apparatuses, deprived of life's most fundamental things, deported, exiles, refugees. . . . Even

though distant from you geographically, we are very close to you. So close as a matter of fact, so as to be the reverse side of your own situation. We are your neighbors. Do not turn a deaf ear to Central America's cry. Do not walk by on the other side, even if it is to go to church. Do not be afraid to contaminate yourselves by taking up our cause. Rather, listen to Jesus' word, "inasmuch as you did it to my smallest brothers and sisters, you did it to me" (Mt. 25:31ff.).

100. *What Have You Done to Your Brother?*
What have you done to these peoples? What have you done to Central America? The blood of this Central American Abel that flows from the veins of 200,000 dead, of numberless martyrs, cries out to heaven and speaks to the U.S. Congress, to the European conquistador, to brothers and sisters unwilling in their lack of concern to get involved.

101. *Opt for the Rebel Poor*
God opted for the poor to liberate them, moving them to seek their own liberation. You too, opt for the poor and against poverty. Rise up against the situation of the poor and fight to destroy the mechanisms that bring it about. Make a political option for freeing the poor, and then translate that option into active participation with them in overcoming the system that generates poverty. Opt for the rebellion of the poor and for the poor rebels, the uncomfortable poor who claim their rights and denounce the privileges of the few. Recognize these poor peoples who have become protagonists in their own history and are calling for their own self-determination as their right, not as charity or a goodwill gesture.

102. *Provincial Christianity Is Not Possible Anymore*
It is no longer possible to be a Christian shut up in the narrow confines of one's own community, or country. Today the only way to be consistent in our Christianity is to take seriously our historical international responsibility with regard to our world neighbors. The cosmos is our home. The world is our family. The peoples are our neighbor. The world is our responsibility. Collective history is our task. It is there that we must make our passionate cry, "Come, Lord Jesus!"

PART III

Acting Today

Ecumenical Solidarity Means
Being Neighbor to Those Who Fight for Life

103. After analyzing our difficult but hope-laden situation in Central America and how it is moving toward a process of peaceful solutions to the structural conflicts that we have pointed out; and

Having carried out extensive theological think-sessions in which theologians, priests, pastors and church lay leaders of the ecumenical movement in Mesoamerica took part:

We want, in this part of our document, to lay out a series of proposals directed at Christian communities in Central America and in the entire world. We present you these proposals, brothers and sisters, with a sense of urgency and for the purpose of contributing toward achieving peace for the Central American peoples and for strengthening the process of their legitimate struggle for justice, equality and human freedom. As Christians we feel ourselves called upon by our Lord to work with a prophetic spirit in this effort, faithful to the cause of the poor and oppressed which is the Kingdom of God's cause.

104. This is the challenge in Central America that calls for a response from us, and which from our context we place before you, Christians and persons of goodwill the world over. We have described for you here the prolonged war which we are still living through, and which we hope will soon cease, because the peoples have an inalienable right to peace and life. We have strongly affirmed, too, that this is no haphazard war, but rather that it is the culmination of a struggle that Central America's people have carried on against their exploiters for five centuries. The war of the last ten years should be understood as an intensification of that longer struggle. However, we wish to emphasize that the Central American peoples are peaceful peoples and have tried to lead lives of peace and social equality throughout their history. It was the colonization that gave rise to our structural violence, and this, in turn, has been exacerbated in this century by U.S. imperialism. Our peoples' longing and the meaning of all their struggle is to put an end to this violence and to any kind of aggression that destroys life and the future, and to open up for themselves a road for new spiritual and material transformation that will lead to the creation of a new community.

105. Dear brothers and sisters, we have understood this struggle from the perspective of the faith that the poor have in the God of life as a moment of grace, an occasion for saving these peoples who have been subjugated for centuries, as a "Kairos" that must not be ignored, since if we disdain this call from the Lord today, it may not come again for many generations.

106. For this reason, we are exhorting each other and appealing to the "neighborliness" of our brothers and sisters. We ask for, we demand, your solidarity for a cause that we believe is God's cause and the cause of his Kingdom. We urge your compassion for the innocent suffering of thousands upon thousands of victims of repression in this nerve center of our continent. We ask for your prayers for and accompaniment of all these people of God.

107. Dear sisters and brothers, so that we can work together for the cause of peace, justice and life for the peoples of Central America, we propose some ways of identifying with them around which we can all organize and act ecumenically.

Challenges for Our Communities in Central America

108. 1. In recent years we have become aware of more concrete experiences in developing an ecumenical spirit in the Christian communities of Central America. Ecumenical projects that have grown out of experience and that help to create peace, justice and freedom for our churches and people are very valuable. We want to encourage each other to cultivate this spirit with grated dedication, to avoid divisions and factionalisms on our part, to foment ecumenical communication and cooperation in our area and in all of Latin America. It is urgent that we coordinate our actions in all phases of church and social life more effectively.

109. 2. We have to confess that for many years we have continued to be indifferent to the pain, suffering and death of the poor, even in our own communities. We reaffirm our firm commitment to the poor, to their struggle for justice, peace and liberation, in this moment of grace. Only in this way does our faith, the proclamation of Jesus' Gospel and communion, make any sense.

110. 3. Peoples' movements to struggle for peace, justice and reconciliation have sprung up in our area. We feel that we ought to support these movements with greater commitment, at the same time that we keep alive the spirit and the flame that gave rise to the "evangelical insurrection" and that have reactivated prophetic activity, in the church, and its discernment of how to be faithful to God's mission.

Urgent Demands on the U.S. Government

111. 4. We demand that the U.S. government completely halt its economic and military support of the counterrevolution in Nicaragua and obey the ruling of the International Court of Justice of June, 1986, that condemned U.S. aggression against Nicaragua and demanded, in addition to its cessation, an indemnization for the consequences of its attacks on civilian communities which caused death and economic destruction. We ask the churches, Christians and solidarity movements in the U.S. to continue to exert pressure for an end to this criminal terrorism action, and that in its place a policy of cooperation and peace for Nicaragua and Central America be developed.

112. 5. We demand that the government and Congress of the United States respect the Republic of Panama's sovereignty and return the canal to it, fulfilling the Torrijos-Carter agreements in every detail.

We urge the democratic governments and peoples of Latin America to express their solidarity with the Panamanian people in their struggle to attain authentic sovereignty.

113. 6. We demand that the United States government withdraw both North American and counterrevolutionary troops from Honduras' territory and respect that country's sovereignty.

114. 7. We demand that the U.S. and Israel and all countries of the world suspend military and police aid to the governments of Guatemala and El Salvador whose armies are waging war against their own suffering peoples, causing thousands of dead and displaced. We ask as well that the organization of United Nations retain its special rappateur in Guatemala for the purpose of documenting the systematic violation of human rights in that country.

Requests Addressed to the Latin American Governments, the United Nations and Other Multilateral Organizations

115. 8. We call upon the Central American governments to carry out the Esquipulas II agreements faithfully, especially with regard to security, democratization, respect for human rights, voluntary repatriation and economic integration. We recommend to the governments of the area that they follow through on the Contadora process in those areas not covered by the Esquipulas II accords.

116. 9. We send an urgent call to the peoples of Latin America and to their respective governments to maintain and increase their solidarity with the Central American cause, viewing it as their own.

117. 10. We send an urgent call to the governments, multilateral development and humanitarian organizations and ecumenical organizations for development to carry out coordinated actions that will contribute toward social and economic reconstruction, as well as to take immediate actions toward alleviating the present economic crisis and famine that threaten the countries of our area. We ask governments, churches and solidarity movements to offer all the aid that our common humanity requires us to give to the Central American refugees that arrive in their countries.

118. 11. We propose that the Organization of the United Nations and the Organization of American States set in motion a concrete process of steps toward the dismantling of foreign military bases in Central America, Belize, Panama and the Caribbean countries, declaring the region a peace zone and respecting it as such.

An Appeal to Churches and Christians Worldwide

119. 12. We ask all the churches of the world, but especially those of Rome, Spain, Portugal, England, the United States and the Latin American countries to hold penitential celebrations of great prominence on the occasion of the 500th anniversary of Latin American subjugation, committing themselves clearly before their governments to its emancipation.

120. 13. We request the churches of the United States and Canada to promote actions of civil disobedience, even going to the extreme that led our brother, Brian Willson, to sacrifice his legs in attempting to halt a military train and restrain the U.S.'s warlike policy against Central America. We recognize the tremendous solidarity that the churches and people of the United States feel for Central America, but we want to tell them that the struggle is a long and painful one, and it has just begun. We urge them to keep up interchange and ecumenical cooperation with Central America to get better acquainted with our situation, and to support our peoples in their noble struggle for Peace and Life.

121. 14. We also ask the churches and Christians of the whole world, and particularly those of Latin America, to carry out prayers, vigils, services, processions and other appropriate intercessory actions for Central America, every year on the anniversary of our brother Oscar Arnulfo Romero's martyrdom (March 24, 1980), as well as at other opportune moments.

The Urgent Need for a New Order with Justice and Peace

122. 15. We concretely ask the General Assembly of the UN, multilateral finance organizations, the World Bank, the International Monetary Fund and the governments of the advanced nations to write off the Third World's foreign debt because it was acquired unjustly and because, among other reasons, the real flow of benefits from the Third World to the rich countries exceeds the entire amount of the debt.

123. 16. We also call upon all the governments of the world urgently to take up the task of creating a new international economic order that will permit the poor countries to get out of their situation of poverty and lead to a process of integrated development with justice and dignity while maintaining respect for the integrity of creating and promoting peace.

124. Dear sisters and brothers, we sign this *Kairos Central America* document in the name of Christ and of our people. We reaffirm, together with you, our intentions of praying, working and struggling toward carrying out of the proposals made herein, so that peace can come to our Central American peoples and to the world. We pray that the grace of God's Spirit accompany our struggle for the Kingdom.

Study Questions for *Kairos Central America*

(*Note*: a full study guide to *Kairos Central America* has been prepared by the Inter-Religious Task Force on Central America, and is available from 475 Riverside Drive, Room 563, New York, NY 10115. It contains material for six sessions, along with appendices that provide further documents and resources for group use. The price is $6.90 including postage.)

Introduction

1. What does it mean to say that "Central America's 'Kairos' arises from 464 years of struggle, agony and hope"? How has "the United States' neocolonial and interventionist policy" contributed to this? (5)

Part I: The Reality We Live In

1. What are the characteristics of "the economic war against the majorities" waged by "the forces of institutionalized violence"? What role has the United States played in this ongoing aggression? (9-21)

2. Trace the historical development of U.S. domination in Central America. Discuss the claim that "militarism continues to be the spinal column of U.S. policy for dominating the area." (22-28)

3. How have "the peoples' struggles" and U.S. policy led to "diametrically opposite" interpretations? (29-34)

5. What has been the role of Christians within the peoples' movements? (35-40)

Part II: Seeing This Historic Hour from a Perspective of Faith

1. What resources are supplied by the words and deeds of Jesus, belief in God, and "the utopia of the Kingdom"? (41-44)

2. What does it mean to signal "the people become subjects of history" as the preeminent "Sign of the Kingdom"? How is this shift from "object" to "subject" receiving expression? (45-49)

3. Reflect on the other "signs of the Kingdom." (50-63) What mood characterizes them? What is the "challenge of martyrdoms"?

Why is the "God of Western Christian Society" at such odds with "the God who is truly Christian"? What criteria lead to such judgments?

4. How are "temporal progress" and "growth in God's Kingdom" related to one another? (62-63)

5. In the Central American context what is "the sin against the Holy Spirit"? (64-67) How is this embodied in the political policies of North Americans, and in "fundamentalist apocalyptic theology"?

6. In what ways and for what reasons do the writers of the document understand themselves to be part of the problem as well as part of the solution, and to accept the need for self-criticism? (68-72)

7. How do we manipulate the defense of "democracy" and human rights for our own ends? (72-76)

8. Compare the indictments in this document and the South African document of inadequate treatments of "violence" and "reconciliation" as means of maintaining power over oppressed groups.

9. What are the Central American ingredients in an understanding of *kairos*? (84-88) Comment on the specifics of para. 87.

10. How is "the option for the poor" a response to a *kairos*-situation? (89-91) Is the "either/or" in para. 91 justified?

11. How are the "nourishing of hope" and "being radical" interrelated?

12. Itemize the challenges the document poses for those of us in the United States (95-102). How accurate is the charge that we are among those most responsible for the 200,000 deaths and the decimation of Central America's political, economic, social and religious life?

13. In what ways *specifically* could we in the United States "opt for the rebel poor"? Can we avoid "provincial Christianity"? (101-102)

Part III: Acting Today

1. Rehearse again the reasons for the sense of urgency and the need for solidarity. (103-7)

2. What demands do the writers place upon themselves? (108-10)

3. What demands do they place on our government and other "outside" groups? (111-18) Some of the historical situations cited in these paragraphs have changed since the document was written. Does this fact alter the responsibility of the United States for ongoing injustice in the region? Do you agree that foreign military bases should be removed?

4. Some specifics: (119-24) How could we participate in "penitential celebrations" in 1992 marking the 500th anniversary of the so-called "discovery" of the New World, and in annual services to remember the martyrdom of Archbishop Romero? How could we work for the writing off of "the Third World's foreign debt" and the creation of a "new international economic order"?

5. At the end of the study reflect again on reasons why the so-called "secular" topics treated in the document are legitimate material for *church* reflection.

The Road to Damascus

Kairos and Conversion

[Africa, Central America, Asia]

Introduction

In solidarity with many Christians in Central America, the writers of *The Road to Damascus* issued their text on July 19, 1989, the tenth anniversary of the triumph of the Sandinista revolution in Nicaragua. The document was in process of being written long before that, however, and represents the fruit of over two and a half years of discussions, meetings and draftings. The logistics of communication during this time were complicated by the enormous geographical distances separating the participants. But as a result of their tenacity, the document reflects the thinking not just of one country (as in the case of South Africa) or one region (as in the case of Central America), but of countries as far-flung as Korea, the Philippines and Namibia, in addition to South Africa and the Central American countries of El Salvador, Guatemala and Nicaragua. The document thus reflects the concerns of Christians from seven countries and three continents. As the Preamble states, hundreds of people were involved in the preparation, and thousands of those to whom it was circulated agreed to sign it.

Although the document contains its full share of social and historical analysis, it focuses particularly on a struggle going on *within the churches* between "two antagonistic forms of Christianity," one of which represents a deep commitment to the liberation of the poor, while the other (assuming different forms in different countries) seeks to use the church and its theology as a safety blanket for the rich and powerful. The theme of "conversion," so powerful in the imagery of the title, refers not only to the need for continuous conversion on the part of the signatories, but also the conversion of those who use Christian faith to give sanction to the evils of the status quo.

The Road to Damascus

Kairos and Conversion

Contents

Preamble

We, the signatories of this document, are Christians from different church traditions in seven different nations: the Philippines, South Korea, Namibia, South Africa, El Salvador, Nicaragua and Guatemala. What we have in common is not only a situation of violent political conflict, but also the phenomenon of Christians on both sides of the conflict. This is accompanied by the development of a Christian theology that sides with the poor and the oppressed and the development of a Christian theology that sides with the oppressor. This is both a scandal and a crisis that challenges the Christian people of our countries.

Although the phenomenon is much the same in each of our countries, the two antagonistic forms of Christianity are referred to with a variety of different names: liberation theology, black theology, feminist theology, minjung theology, theology of struggle, the Church of the poor, the progressive church, basic Christian communities, on the one hand; and the religious right, right-wing Christianity, state theology, the theology of reconciliation, the neo-Christendom movements and anticommunist evangelicals, on the other hand. In each of our nations we shall have to spell out exactly which groups of Christians we are referring to. Whatever difference of terminology there may be, the conflict and division among Christians is basically the same in each of our countries.

The purpose of this document is not simply to deplore the divisions among Christians or to exhort both sides to seek unity. We wish to lay bare the historical and political roots of the conflict (Chapter 1), to affirm the faith of the poor and the oppressed Christians in our countries (Chapter 2), to condemn the sins of those who oppress, exploit, persecute and kill people (Chapter 3), and to call to conversion those who have strayed from the truth of Christian faith and commitment (Chapter 4). The time has come for us to take a stand and to speak out.

The road ahead is like the road to Damascus along which Saul was travelling to persecute the first generation of Christians. It was along this road that he heard the voice of Jesus calling him to conversion. We are all in continuous need of self-criticism and conversion. But now the time has come for a decisive turnabout on the part of those groups and individuals who have consciously or unconsciously compromised their Christian faith for political, economic and selfish reasons.

Hundreds of Christians have been involved in the preparation of this document, and thousands of us have chosen to sign it. Extensive research and consultation within each of our countries and weeks of dialogue between representatives from the seven countries were conducted over a period of two and a half years. The results of all this work are presented here as a proclamation of faith and a call to conversion.

CHAPTER ONE

The Roots of Our Conflict

1. As Christians, we look at our situation with eyes that have read the Bible stories. According to the Bible, violent conflict began when Cain killed his brother Abel despite the fact that they had just offered sacrifices together to the same God (Gen 4:3-8). Israel was born as a people of God in struggle against the power of Egypt. It had to confront the great empires of ancient times, the Assyrians, the Babylonians, the Greeks and the Romans. The prophets were often in conflict with the kings of Israel when they saw that the people were treated unjustly. Jesus preached a message that incurred the ire of the religious authorities, who handed him over to the Roman procurator to be crucified.

2. The early Christians were considered a threat by the Roman empire; they were persecuted and martyred. Then in the 4th century, under Emperor Constantine, Christianity became the official religion of the empire. In the hands of the ruling powers it became a weapon for legitimising the expansion of the empire and, later, the colonisation of peoples.

Colonialism

3. Except in the case of Korea, which was colonised by Japan, the European nations that colonised our countries pride themselves on being Christian. Conquest and evangelisation, colonisation and the building of churches advanced together. The cross blessed the sword which was responsible for the shedding of our people's blood. The sword imposed the faith and protected the churches, sharing power and wealth with them.

4. As a result of "discovery and conquest", millions of people have been killed; indigenous populations have been eliminated; entire civilisations and cultures have been destroyed. Millions have been enslaved, uprooted from their native land, deculturised and deprived of their wealth and resources. Women and children have been victims of additional and distinct oppression. Natural resources have been exploited and abused to such an extent that they cannot be replenished.

5. One of the most serious and lasting legacies of European colonialism is racism. In South Africa it has been institutionalised and legalised in the form of the notorious system of apartheid.

People against Colonialism

6. The history of our people is not only a history of oppression and suffering; it is also a history of struggle. The first stories of resistance come from the indigenous people and communities. The colonisers had superior weapons and the indigenous communities often fought separately instead of together, but they resisted, sometimes to the very last member of the community. Others withdrew more deeply into the mountains to preserve what was left unconquered by the invaders.

7. From within the womb of colonialism, those who were initially conquered eventually rose in rebellion, and in some cases overthrew colonial rule through revolution. There were many battles and few lasting victories, but the prophets and martyrs of the people established a tradition of resistance.

8. Although Christianity was part and parcel of colonial rule, Christians were also to be found on the side of the people who fought against colonialism. In Latin America, during the first centuries of colonisation, missionaries and even bishops added their own to the voices of protest, to the extent of denying the Spanish crown the right to expropriate the land of indigenous people and to put them under foreign authorities. In Korea Christians fought for national independence against Japanese colonialism.

Western Imperialism

9. Today, most Third World countries are no longer colonies, but we are still dominated by one or more imperial power—the United States, Japan and Western Europe. Their web of economic control includes an unfair international trade system, multinational companies that monopolise strategic sections of our economy, economic policies dictated by lending banks and government together with the International Monetary Fund and the World Bank. Even technology is used as a tool for domination. The staggering size of Third World debt is only one dramatic sign of our subordination to imperialism.

10. In some of our countries imperialism violates national sovereignty by establishing military bases with nuclear weapons that endanger our people's lives. Various methods of political intervention subvert our independence, usually with the cooperation of local rulers. Our educational system, mass media, religious and cultural institutions reproduce a subservient colonial mentality; this is reinforced by Western habits of consumption.

11. Imperialism uses the tactic of divide and rule. It supports governments that discriminate against people and treat them unjustly because of their race or colour. It reinforces sexism and the subordination of women. It sometimes widens the divisions even among the elite, but more often it seeks to unite the ruling elite against the people. In most countries this leads to the establishment of what is today called the *national security state.*

12. The effects of imperialism upon the Third World form a litany of woes: our children die of malnutrition and disease, there are no jobs for those who want to work, families break up to pursue employment abroad, peasants and indigenous communities are displaced from their land, most urban dwellers have to live in unsanitary slums, many women have to sell their bodies, too many die without having lived a life that human persons deserve. We also suffer because of the plunder of our natural resources, and then we ourselves are being blamed for it.

People against Imperialism

13. The tradition of popular resistance lives on in our countries. Even though most of our ruling elite collude with imperialism to deceive and divide the people, groups and communities manage to reflect critically on their oppression and organise themselves. Communities of peasants and indigenous people, workers and slum dwellers—men, women and children—struggle for their own immediate needs and also for shared long-term issues. In much the same way, students, youth and teachers, church people and cultural workers, doctors, nurses, lawyers and members of other professions, including some business people, become part of the mass democratic movement.

14. As this movement becomes more widespread and organised, the power and wisdom of ordinary people develops and deepens. They recall lessons from history, learn from their mistakes and achievements, and experience solidarity. They exchange insights about the nature of imperialism and its many disguises. Going beyond protest and resistance, they assume responsibility for proposing and pursuing a people's alternative to the present system. They do not have illusions that the struggle will be easy or quick, but also do not shirk sacrifice because they have hope.

15. This movement of organised and conscious people marks the coming of age of a new historical subject. As we exchange our stories not only within our countries but among different countries, we also learn the many names we give to this new creation—the people, *el pueblo, minjung, ang sambayanan.*

16. As Third World people, we focus on Western imperialism and what is called North-South relations, but we are aware of other important conflicts in the world. There is the East-West conflict between industrial capitalist countries and socialist countries. There are conflicts within capitalist countries and among capitalist countries; the same is true of socialist countries.

17. Western imperialism tries to force our struggle for national liberation into an East-West framework. Let us be clear that we know about the wrongdoings of the East, both within socialist countries themselves and in their relation to other Third World countries. But what we experience directly is domination by the West, and we do not want to be drawn into the East-West conflict.

18. Socialist countries are admitting their mistakes and addressing the need for reforms. The United States and the Soviet Union both declare that they want to slow down and even reverse the arms race, and talk of negotiations to solve regional conflicts. All these are welcome pronouncements. Ironically, just when there is talk of more peaceful coexistence between East and West, our countries in the South experience increased hostile attacks from the West.

Low-Intensity Conflict and Total War

19. Colonial and imperial powers have reacted to the people's resistance by devising different counter-insurgency programmes. Faced with the emergence of Third World people as new historical subjects, they have developed what they consider a more sophisticated response. It has different names—low-intensity conflict (LIC), low-intensity war, total war, total strategy, total security.

20. For the imperialists, it might be low-intensity conflict, but for the Third World people it is total war. LIC uses all military weapons, short of nuclear arms. It employs not just rifle infantry, but artillery, helicopter gunships, armoured vehicles like casspirs in South Africa and Namibia and armadillos in Central America; it does not hesitate to bomb suspected rebel areas. It organises paramilitary groups, death squads and vigilantes to divide and destroy unarmed communities and organisations of the people.

21. Unlike traditional regular warfare, total war places a premium on psychological and ideological war. In Namibia and South Africa, this is called "winning hearts and minds" or WHAM. The Santa Fe Document calls it "cultural war". It tries to discredit all those who work for change by calling them "communists", while trying to present the government as democratic. In highly repressive and polarised situations, it promotes reformist alternatives, or a "third force". This total strategy includes the misuse of Christianity as a religious legitimation for the West.

Christians in Conflict

22. The misuse of Christianity in the ideological war is imperialism's response to an earlier development—the good news of Christian participation in the suffering and struggle of the people.

23. Some Christians started by immersing themselves in communities of the oppressed and then came to understand their faith as a commitment to solidarity. For other Christians, involvement came as their response to an imperative of faith, the fruit of reflection in basic Christian communities. However different their paths may have been, their participation developed into a more organised and conscious direction. They took up whatever tasks needed to be done within the people's movement, but they also sought to release the power and resources of their faith and church to serve the poor.

24. This new development has caused grave concern in the highest circles of imperialist leaders. The organised and conscious presence of Christians in the people's movement is not only one more addition to the ranks of those who struggle against the system of domination; it weakens the capacity of imperialism to use Christianity to defend the Empire.

25. No wonder then that formal proposals for a systematic attack on theology of liberation have been presented to the president of the United States, as in the Santa Fe Documents I and II. New institutions have been established to develop a theology that defends imperialism. Joint projects are launched with some Third World governments and security agencies to infiltrate the Church, coopt conservative Christians and "neutralise" progressive ones. Christianity is interpreted to suit these purposes while the theology of liberation is accused of being political.

26. Christian faith has now been introduced into the political conflict. Both oppressor and oppressed seek religious legitimation. Both sides invoke the name of God and of Jesus Christ, and Christians are found on both sides of the political conflict in most of our seven countries.

27. Nor does the matter end there. The political conflict has now entered into the Churches. The Church itself has become a *site of struggle*. Some sectors of the Church align themselves with the status quo and defend it passionately, while others align themselves with the oppressed and struggle for change. There are yet others who claim to be neutral. In fact neutrality plays into the hands of those in power because it enables them to continue and to discredit the Christians who oppose them. Neutrality is an indirect way of supporting the status quo.

28. There is nothing new about religious conflict as such. Christians or believers in the God of the Bible have been on opposing sides in political conflicts before. What is new today is the intensity of the conflict and the awareness we have of it. Never before have we been so conscious of the political implications of Christian faith. This religious conflict is not a mere academic debate, it is a matter of life and death. What is at stake is the future of justice, peace, freedom and the glory of God.

29. The conflict among Christians raises some very serious questions which we shall have to address in the rest of this document:

Is the God invoked by both sides the same God?

Is God on both sides?

If not, on whose side is God?

What has been revealed to us about God in Jesus?

CHAPTER TWO

The Faith of the Poor

30. The God whom the missionaries preached was a God who blessed the powerful, the conquerors, the colonisers. This God demanded resignation in the face of oppression and condemned re-belliousness and insubordination. All that was offered to us by this God was an interior and other-worldly liberation. It was a God who dwelt in heaven and in the Temple but not in the world.

31. The Jesus who was preached to us was barely human. He seemed to float above history, above all human problems and conflicts. He was pictured as a high and mighty king or emperor who ruled over us, even during his earthly life, from the heights of his majestic throne. His approach to the poor was therefore thought of as condescending. He condescended to make the poor the objects of his mercy and compassion without sharing their oppression and their struggles. His death had nothing to do with historical conflicts, but was a human sacrifice to placate an angry God. What was preached to us was a completely other-worldly Jesus who had no relevance to this life.

32. These were the images of God and Jesus that we inherited from our conquerors and the missionaries who accompanied them. In some cases these beliefs were imposed upon us at the point of the sword, and some of our ancestors were forcibly baptised. In the case of Korea, European missionaries came without colonisation. It was only later that we discovered that this God and this Jesus had been formed in the image and likeness of European kings, emperors and conquerors.

33. Gradually our experience of poverty and oppression began to raise questions for us: Why does God allow us to suffer so much? Why does God always side with the rich and the powerful? Some of us began to see that these questions were also raised in the psalms and in the book of Job, which refused to accept any easy answers. Was poverty and oppression really the will of God?

34. In time we began to realise that we could never expect justice from our oppressors. After many years of protest and pleading we began to take responsibility for our own liberation. We began to organise ourselves and became a people, the subjects of our own history, *el pueblo, minjung. Minjung* is the Korean word for the people as opposed to the ruling powers when they become conscious of themselves as subjects who can decide for themselves instead of being mere objects to be ruled and governed.

35. The Christians who were part of this development began to read the Bible with new eyes. We were no longer dependent upon the interpretations of our oppressors.

36. What we discovered was that Jesus was one of us. He was born in poverty. He did not become incarnate as a king or nobleman but as one of the poor and oppressed. He took sides with the poor, supported their cause and blessed them. On the other hand, he condemned the rich: "Blessed are you who are poor" (Lk 6:20); "Woe to you who are rich" (Lk 6:24). He even described his mission as the liberation of the downtrodden (Lk 4:18). That was the very opposite of what we had been taught.

37. At the heart of Jesus' message was the coming of the Reign of God. We discovered that Jesus had promised the Reign of God to the poor: "Yours is the Reign of God" (Lk 6:20), and that the good news about the coming of God's Reign was supposed to be good news for the poor (Lk 4:18).

38. The Reign of God is not simply a way of speaking about the next world. The Reign of God is this world completely transformed in accordance with God's plan. It is like the Jubilee year of Leviticus 25 when all those who are living in slavery will be set free, when all debts will be cancelled and when the land will be restored to those from whom it was stolen. The Reign of God begins in this life but stretches out beyond this life. It is transcendent and eschatological without being unconcerned about the problems and suffering of the poor in this life.

39. In preaching the Reign of God Jesus was prophesying the coming of a new world order. This brought him into conflict with the status quo of his time, the religious and political authorities. They found his preaching "subversive". That is why they conspired to kill him.

40. Jesus was and still is the Word of God, the true image of God. The poor and the oppressed Christians of today, together with those who have taken an option for the poor, can now see the true face of God in the poor Jesus—persecuted and oppressed like them. God is not an almighty oppressor. The God we see in the face of Jesus is the God who hears the cries of the poor and who leads them across the sea and the desert to the promised land (Ex 3:17). The true God is the God of the poor who is angry about injustice in the world, vindicates the poor (Ps 103:6), pulls down the mighty from their thrones and lifts up the lowly (Lk 1:52). This is the God who will judge all human beings according to what they have done or not done for the hungry, the thirsty, the naked, the sick and those in prison (Mt 25:31-46).

41. We are grateful to God for the grace that has enabled us to rediscover God in Jesus Christ. "I bless you, Father, for hiding these things from the learned and the clever and revealing them to mere children" (Lk 10:21). It is by the Spirit of God that we have been able to see what the learned and the clever were not able to see. We no longer believe in the God of the powerful and we want no gods except the God who was in Jesus. "I am Yahweh your God, who brought you out of the land of Egypt, out of the house of slavery. You shall have no gods except me" (Ex 20:1-2).

42. With this new faith in Jesus, we can now begin to read the signs of our times, discern the presence of the risen Jesus in our midst, appreciate the action of the Holy Spirit and see our present conflict with new eyes. We are no longer surprised to discover that the followers of Jesus are crucified and killed. Now we hear God's voice, especially in the cry of the poor, in the cry of pain and protest, of despair and hope.

43. God is on the side of the poor, the oppressed, the persecuted. When this faith is proclaimed and lived in a situation of political conflict between the rich and the poor, and when the rich and the powerful reject this faith and condemn it as heresy, we can read the signs and discern something more than a crisis. We are faced with a *kairos,* a moment of truth, a time for decision, a time of grace, a God-given opportunity for conversion and hope.

CHAPTER THREE

Our Prophetic Mission

44. Throughout history, we Christians have often been deaf to God's voice and blind to God's presence in people. This lack of faith has prevented us from exercising the prophetic mission that Jesus has given us. We have often been silent instead of denouncing injustice and oppression. Instead of working for justice and liberation, we have often remained uninvolved.

45. How shall we explain this silence and uninvolvement, this blindness and unbelief? For some of us, the reason lies in a life that is not confronted by the suffering and struggle of the poor, and therefore the choice of a convenient God who does not challenge us to take part in a movement for change. For others, however, the reason lies in a choice of privilege and power, and a *conscious* defence of the status quo. In many cases, it includes taking part in attacks against movements for change, in repression and the killing of the poor.

46. For such people, it is not simply an inability to see and hear; it is a refusal to see and hear. It is not merely lack of faith in the God of life; it is the worship of a false god—the sin of idolatry.

47. Although we are conscious of our own sins, we must raise our voice in the denunciation of this sin. It is a sin that serves the total war being waged against the people, leading to the death and destruction of our communities.

48. The sin of idolatry lies at the heart of the imperialism of money. In choosing to serve the idols of death rather than the God of life,

Christianity is used as a weapon against the people. Idolatry leads Christians to other sins—heresy and apostasy, hypocrisy and blasphemy.

Idolatry

49. Idolatry is the sin of worshipping or being subservient to someone or something which is not God, treating some created thing as if it were a god. "They worshipped and served the creature instead of the Creator" (Rm 1:25). In the Old Testament Moses and the prophets condemned the worship of the golden calf, the Baals and other idols made by human hands (Ex 20:4-5; Ps 115:4). In New Testament times the principal form of idolatry was the worship of mammon (Mt 6:24; Lk 16:13).

50. The same is true for us today. In our countries, the worship of money, power, privilege and pleasure has certainly replaced the worship of God. This form of idolatry has been organised into a system in which consumerist materialism has been enthroned as a god. Idolatry makes things, especially money and property, more important than people. It is *anti-people.*

51. Because the idol is anti-people, it *demands absolute submission and blind obedience.* The idols we read about in the Bible make their followers into slaves, prisoners or robots depriving them of freedom. Subservience to money dehumanises people. Profits are pursued at the expense of people. The graven image of the god of money today is the national security state that defends the system and demands absolute and blind obedience. In some countries, it is cruel and merciless; in others, it wears a deceptive mask. Those who disobey are punished brutally; those who obey are rewarded with material benefits and security. Idols rule by fear and intimidation or by trying to buy people, to bribe them and seduce them with money.

52. Idolatry is the *denial of all hope for the future.* The idols of the past were worshipped by people who were afraid of change, who wanted things to remain the same, who did not want a future that was different, who found their security in the status quo. The same is true today. Those who benefit from the status quo live in total fear of any real transformation. They are at the service of the status quo and will go to any lengths to make it secure.

53. It was for the sake of *security* that the people of ancient times turned to the Baals and other idols. Today, our oppressors turn to money and military power and to the so-called security forces. But their security is our insecurity. We experience their security as intimidation and repression, terror, rape and murder. Those who turn to the idols for security demand our insecurity as the price that must be paid. They fear us as a threat to their security.

54. Idolatry demands a *scapegoat.* The idolaters believe that some people or groups of people must be blamed for all that goes wrong in a society so that by driving out or killing the scapegoat, they can feel purged and exonerated of their guilt. This is an idolatrous way of dealing with guilt and achieving atonement. Often enough, perfectly innocent people are sacrificed as scapegoats, though it may sometimes happen that the scapegoat is not entirely innocent, like the woman taken in adultery in John 8:2-11.

55. The worshippers of money in our countries use communism or socialism of any kind or even suspected leanings in that direction as their scapegoat. The guilt that they feel and the sins that they commit are projected onto this convenient scapegoat, which then can be blamed for all that is wrong or might go wrong in the future. Thus violence, disregard for human rights, repression and brutality are talked about as the characteristics of communists. It then becomes perfectly justifiable to harass, imprison, torture and even kill them. They have become scapegoats.

56. In this way it also becomes possible to justify the persecution of the Church. Certain people in the Church, progressive groups or, in some places, Church leaders, are labelled "communists", to separate them from other Christians and turn them into scapegoats who can then be discredited, hated, denounced, silenced and even eliminated.

57. The idols demand *human sacrifices.* This is what angered the prophets most of all about the worship of the Baals. Jeremiah deplored the superstitious belief that the gods can only be placated by the sacrifice of children (Jer 19:4-5). Today this is still the most evil dimension of the sin of idolatry in our countries. People, young and old, innocent and defenceless, are being sacrificed to placate mammon—the national security state and international capitalism.

58. We live with the everyday reality of human sacrifice: starving children, deaths in detention, assassinations, massacres and disappearances. The killing of people has become a kind of religious ritual, a necessary part of the total war on people.

59. Idolatry is *fanatical*. It encourages irrational and unrestrained behaviour. We see this in the massacres of people by soldiers, policemen and death squads, *contras* and vigilantes. We see it also in their demented hatred of those who resist and their frenzied persecution of church persons when they protest. It is impossible to be reasonable when you submit to the idols of money, power, privilege and pleasure. The idols create bloodthirsty feelings that the system itself cannot control.

60. Idolatry is a *lie,* and it can only continue by deceiving people more and more. The fundamental lie is making material things more important than people. Scapegoating is a lie. Presenting all real change as communist and therefore atheist is a lie.

61. Idolatry's propaganda is a series of lies. It presents the existing order as the natural order of things and radical change as chaos. It coopts the words that people use to describe their aspirations, like peace, democracy and freedom, and makes them mean something different. Peace comes to mean preserving the status quo. Democracy is used to describe the manipulation of national elections, apartheid elections for local government as in South Africa, or a mechanism to ensure that the majority of the people do not have access to real power. Freedom means giving the rich and powerful the opportunity to exploit and manipulate others. Idolatry disguises the truth and creates a whole culture of lies. Satan, as Jesus says, is the father of lies (Jn 8:44).

Heresy

62. The word *heresy* means *choice*. A heresy is a form of belief that selects some parts of the Christian message and rejects other parts, in such a way that those doctrines which are selected for belief become themselves distorted.

63. The theological justification of apartheid in South Africa has been declared a heresy. It is recognised by most Christians today to be a distortion of God's revelation. But we would like to take this famous declaration further: we denounce all forms of right-wing Christianity as heretical.

64. Right-wing Christianity under whatever name is a way of believing that rejects or ignores parts of God's revelation and selects or distorts other parts in order to support the ideology of the national security state. We are convinced that this heretical choice is made for selfish political purposes, although not all the adherents of right-wing Christianity are necessarily aware of this. Consequently right-wing Christianity is the conscious or unconscious legitimation of idolatry.

65. Right-wing Christianity is being promoted with vigorous and expensive campaigns in all our countries and in almost all Christian traditions: Catholic, Reformed, Lutheran, Anglican, Evangelical and Pentecostal.

66. One of the characteristics of this new heresy is that it denies Christian freedom by insisting upon blind obedience to authority. The famous text from Romans 13 is misused to demand unquestioning and uncritical allegiance to the political authorities who exercise the politics of death and deception. Similarly, in some countries Christians are commanded to submit themselves blindly to the absolute authority of church leaders.

67. Right-wing Christianity replaces Christian responsibility and trust in God with submission to the yoke of slavery. It promotes authoritarianism and domination in the family and society. It often distorts even the authority of the Bible by treating it as a book from heaven that must be obeyed without understanding or critical comprehension. In some countries, this is called fundamentalism. The attempt to find security in blind obedience, absolute certainties and submission to authoritarianism is not faith. It is slavery. "For freedom Christ has set us free; stand fast therefore, and do not submit again to the yoke of slavery" (Gal 5:1).

68. Another characteristic of right-wing religion is that it takes some of the valid distinctions made by Christianity, e.g., between body and soul, material and spiritual, this world and the next, politics and religion, the profane and the sacred, society and the individual and turns them into antagonistic *dualisms*. It creates polarisation and antagonism between the body and the soul, the material and the spiritual. This is against Christian teaching since the Bible reveals only one God, creator of the material and the spiritual, the individual and the social. We must not "put asunder what God has put together".

69. It is not without reason that right-wing Christians believe in antagonistic dualisms. It prevents the spiritual from influencing their material lives, it keeps God out of their political and economic interests. They say that they are only interested in the soul, but in fact they are very concerned about the political and economic status quo. They want to preserve it at all costs because it benefits them. They say we must keep religion out of politics but invoke a kind of religion that supports the status quo. They reduce salvation to that of the soul only.

70. This leads to an otherworldly interpretation of the Bible. Everything in the Bible that refers to material possessions, wealth and poverty, oppression and liberation is distorted and made to refer only to other-worldly and individualistic concerns. This spiritualistic interpretation of the Bible is reductionist.

71. A further characteristic of right-wing Christianity is that it is fanatically *anti-communist*. It one-sidedly identifies Christianity with capitalist values of individualism and competition while rejecting the Christian values of equality and cooperation, saying that these are communist and socialist values. Communism, whatever real faults it may have, is then used as a *scapegoat*. The war against communism is treated as a holy war or crusade. Christian values like loving your enemy, forgiving seventy times seven times, compassion, solidarity and calling the sinner to conversion are conveniently forgotten once a person or group is labelled "communist" or "subversive".

Apostasy

72. Apostasy goes much further than heresy. It abandons the Christian faith altogether. In the past, those who apostatised from the Christian faith gave up the name "Christian". But today it would not be strategic for the worshippers of the idol to admit that they are no longer Christians. For convenience they still call themselves Christians and continue formally professing the Christian faith, but in fact they no longer believe, much less live, the gospel of Jesus Christ.

73. That they are not just heretical Christians but apostates becomes unmistakably clear when they begin to *persecute* the Church. They discredit priests and pastors, nuns and theologians, church leaders and Christian communities, harass them, sometimes imprison them, torture and kill them. When the Church and its theology is seen as a dangerous threat to the national security state and when the Church becomes a target for national security strategy, then it is not just a question of heresy but of apostasy.

74. In some of our countries military chaplains are sent to schools to explain the total war against the people. They arrange camps and conferences for church youth and Sunday school teachers; military men are specially trained to take over catechism classes. Alternative councils of churches are set up, alternative church leaders and churches are promoted to support the national security state.

75. This persecution of Christians also involves vicious attacks upon liberation theology. Right-wing sects are promoted in order to undermine and divide those Churches that take the side of the poor. This is part of an imperialist strategy that does not even bother to keep itself secret; it is spelled out clearly for Latin America in the Santa Fe Documents I and II.

Hypocrisy

76. Jesus issued many strong condemnations of the hypocrisy of the scribes and Pharisees. They did not always practise what they preached. They were not in reality what they appeared to be in public, they were whited sepulchres. Because they were more concerned about their popularity and their reputations than about the truth, they became too cowardly to speak out about the real evils in their society. They strained out gnats while swallowing camels and saw the splinter in someone's eye while overlooking the plank in their own eyes (Mt 23:24; 7:5).

77. Is it not true that some Christians and church leaders in our countries are like those scribes and Pharisees? They are very cautious and "prudent" and do not wish to rock the boat. They are either part of the rich and powerful or afraid of them. Even when there are obvious cases of injustice, they do not speak out or do something about it. When hundreds or even thousands "disappear", it is especially hypocritical for church leaders to maintain their silence. We know that in some cases, this silence is even worse than hypocrisy—it is a mask for their complicity in the "dirty war".

78. There are those who claim to be nonpartisan and talk of keeping the balance, but they betray their partisanship by criticising mainly those who question the status quo. They speak of reconciliation and patience, but address this mainly to the victims of the system and the powerless. They promote reforms as a "third way", but restrict people's participation to traditional forms. They profess commitment to democracy, but do not wish the people to exercise power effectively. They warn against the dangers of politicising the Church, but they often compromise the Church through alliances and negotiations with those in power. They accuse progressive Christians of dividing the Church, but in some countries they use their position to force a split between the institutional and the popular Church, even denying that some base communities are part of the Church.

79. There is hypocrisy in the use of double standards, while claiming to have only one. For example, there are those who preach absolute nonviolence, but while they condemn the armed struggle of the people, they seldom question the use of arms against the people. They recognise the right of self-defence when the state invokes it, but not when the people exercise it. In the case of military forces, they uphold the legitimate use of violence and criticise only its abuse; but when it comes to the people's use of arms, they do not make the same distinction. The ideological reasons for such double standards are exposed by what they say about a state that is socialist, anti-imperialist or progressive. Suddenly, they seem to have no problem at all about the use of violence against such states, even indiscriminate violence. This is a clear case of double standards and hypocrisy.

Blasphemy

80. Idolatry is a sin against the first commandment. Of all the sins related to it, none is more scandalous than the sin against the second commandment—blasphemy. "You shall not utter the name of Yahweh your God to misuse it" (Ex 20:7). It is blasphemy to misuse the name of God in defence of imperialism. Theologians of the Institute of Religion and Democracy in the United States of America even compare multinational corporations to the servant of Yahweh. This sin has deadlier consequences when some bishops and priests become military officers, thereby legitimising the armed forces, and when they publicly bless the weapons of war that are used to kill our people, thereby justifying total war as a holy war. In some countries there are priests who are not only chaplains of the military, they even provide spiritual advice to leaders of death squads. To invoke the name of the God of life to justify death and destruction is blasphemy. It is giving scandal to the little ones (Mk 9:42; Lk 17:1-2).

81. In the service of the idols, certain things and persons become sacred. Money and property and, above all, security are sacred. Government and military authorities are like priests of a pseudo-religion. In some countries whites become a sacred people. This too is blasphemy.

82. Blasphemy also takes the form of "satanisation"—attributing the work of the Holy Spirit to the devil. Satanisation refuses to see the God of life in the liberation of the people. It sees the work of liberation as the work of Satan and accuses the people of being possessed by evil spirits. In his time, Jesus was accused of being under the power of Beelzebul precisely when he freed people from evil spirits and healed them. We also remember Jesus' warning about the sin against the Holy Spirit (Mk 3:22-30).

CHAPTER FOUR

The Call to Conversion

83. The most famous conversion story in the New Testament is the story of the apostle Paul on the road to Damascus. Before his conversion, Saul (as he was then called) persecuted those Jews who had been converted to the way of Jesus. He took sides with the Sanhedrin, the chief priests of the Temple, the scribes and the Pharisees, against Jesus and the people who believed in Jesus. In other words, Saul sided with the authorities and the status quo against this new movement that wanted to "turn the world upside down" (Acts 17:6). Saul stood by and approved of the killing of Stephen (Acts 7:58; 8:1). Stephen, like Jesus, was seen as a dangerous threat to the Temple and the Law (Acts 6:14-15). This was more than a religious conflict because the Temple was the centre not only of religious power but also of political and economic power, while the Law was the guarantee that nothing in that society would change. As far as Saul was concerned, Judaism had to be purged of this new movement in its midst. The disciples of Jesus had to be pursued in every town and village, dragged out and stoned like Stephen.

84. "Saul was still breathing threats to slaughter the Lord's disciples" as he travelled down the road to Damascus armed with letters authorising him to arrest any followers of the Way, men or women, that he could find (Acts 9:1-2). Then suddenly it happened. Saul made the startling discovery that he was on the wrong side, that God was on the side of Jesus and that the persecution of the people who followed Jesus was the persecution of Jesus himself.

"Saul, Saul, why do you persecute me?
Who are you, Lord?
I am Jesus whom you are persecuting" (Acts 9:3-5).

85. What was revealed to Saul was that God was not on the side of the religious and political authorities who had killed Jesus. On the contrary, God was on the side of the One who had been crucified as a blasphemer, who had been accused of being possessed by Beelzebul, who had been handed over as a traitor, an agitator, a pretender to the throne of David and a critic of the Temple (Mt 26:62, 65-66; Lk 23:1-2, 5, 13). On the road to Damascus Saul was faced with this conflict between these two images or beliefs about God. He was struck blind by it. It was his kairos. Saul became Paul when he accepted in faith that the true God was in Jesus and that the risen Lord was in the very people whom he had been persecuting.

86. This kairos on the road to Damascus must be taken seriously by all who in the name of God support the persecution of Christians who side with the poor. The call to conversion is loud and clear.

87. We must be converted again and again from the idol of mammon to the worship of the true God. We cannot serve two masters, we cannot serve both God and mammon (Mt 6:24).

88. Beware of false prophets. They come to us disguised as sheep but inside they are wild wolves. We can recognise what they really are by their fruit (Mt 7:15-20). There are false prophets who say there is peace when there is no peace (Jer 6:14; 8:11; Ez 13:10). Hear the prophetic voice of those who are being persecuted and oppressed.

89. God is calling us to abandon the practice of making individuals or groups into scapegoats who can be blamed for the very sins that we ourselves commit. Most of all the practice of using communism as a scapegoat must be exposed and rejected. Communist regimes and movements must be criticised too, but they must not be made into scapegoats.

90. We must take seriously Jesus' accusation of hypocrisy. We cannot sit on the fence and profess neutrality while people are being persecuted, exploited and killed. We cannot remain silent because we fear the authorities and do not want to rock the boat. Jesus calls all hypocrites to conversion.

91. All of us who profess to be followers of Jesus of Nazareth are in continuous need of conversion. While we see clearly the idolatry, the heresy, the hypocrisy and the blasphemy of others, we ourselves need to search our own hearts for remnants of the same sins and for signs of triumphalism, self-righteousness, dogmatism, rigidity, intolerance and sectarianism. There should be no place in our hearts for any kind of complacency.

Conclusion

The particular crisis or kairos that has led us to the writing and signing of this proclamation of faith is the conflict between Christians in the world today. We have wished to make it quite clear that those Christians who side with the imperialists, the oppressors and the exploiters of people are siding with the idolaters who worship money, power, privilege and pleasure. To misuse Christianity to defend oppression is heretical. And to persecute Christians who are oppressed or who side with the oppressed is apostasy—the abandonment of the gospel of Jesus Christ.

What we are dealing with here is not simply a matter of morality or ethics. What is at stake is the true meaning of our Christian faith. Who is God? Where is the true Jesus? It is not those Christians who struggle against oppression who are heretics, but those who support the forces of evil and death. The name of God is being blasphemously misused.

This proclamation was written and signed to give an account of the *hope* that is in us. Like the disciples who travelled along the road to Emmaus we are sometimes tempted to give up hope. As the two disciples say: "Our own hope had been that he (Jesus) would be the one to set Israel free" (Lk 24:21). What they still had to learn from Jesus and what we need to be reminded of again and again is that the way to freedom and salvation is the way of the cross. "Was it not ordained that the Christ should suffer and so enter into his glory?"

(Lk 24:26). There is no cheap solution or liberation. There is no easy road.

Because of our faith in Jesus, we are bold enough to hope for something that fulfills and transcends all human expectations, namely, the Reign of God. We are even called to live with the hope that those who collaborate with the idols of death and those who persecute us today will be converted to the God of life.

None of this can happen, however, without pain, suffering and many deaths. Jesus promises us the Reign of God but he also promises that "they will hand you over to the Sanhedrins and scourge you in their synagogues". "You will be dragged before governors and kings." "Brother (and sister) will betray brother (and sister) to death, and the father his child." "You will be hated by all on account of my name" (Mt 10:17-22).

The disciple cannot be greater than the master, and we are following the path of a crucified Christ. Whatever twists and turns the road might take, be firm and steadfast. The pain we undergo is part of the birthpangs of a new creation.

The experience of our seven countries working together to compile this document over a period of two and a half years has been an example of solidarity. We hope that such examples of cooperation and dialogue will continue, will develop and will be extended for the benefit of all.

Our oppressors organise themselves nationally and internationally. We cannot afford to face the struggle separately. Solidarity is not optional if we are to promote the cause of God in the world. We call on fellow Christians in the Third World, in industrial capitalist countries and in socialist countries to build a network of exchange and cooperation.

July 1989

Study Questions for *The Road to Damascus*

(*Note:* no extensive study guide on *The Road to Damascus* has yet appeared. Groups who have contributed to such a project are urged to send drafts to the Committee of Correspondence noted in Appendix B.)

Chapter One: The Roots of Our Conflict

1. In what ways does the early history of the church (i.e., the transition from being a "threat to the Roman empire" to becoming "the official religion of the empire") reflect our own loss of prophetic challenge and our cooptation by contemporary culture? (2)

2. How did Christianity and "colonialism" become so intertwined? (3-5) What were the reasons for many Christians finally rebelling against this collusion? (6-8)

3. What are some of the baleful effects of the "western imperialism" that replaced "colonialism"? (9-12) In what ways have these effects been legitimated and incorporated into U.S. foreign policy?

4. In what ways have Christians and others challenged the assumptions of imperialism? How has the struggle changed from East vs. West to North vs. South? (13-18)

5. What does it mean to say of a counter-insurgency program that "for the imperialists it might be low-intensity conflict, but for the Third World people it is total war"? (19-21)

6. What are some of the reasons for the wide-scale attacks on liberation theology, both within the church and on the part of the U.S. government? (22-26)

7. How legitimate is the claim of certain Christians to be "neutral" in the midst of political conflict? (27)

8. What is "new" in the current religious struggle, and how has the church become "a site of struggle"? (28)

9. In the light of the history reported in Chapter One, reflect on the four questions with which it closes, as a basis for studying the next chapter. (29)

Chapter Two: The Faith of the Poor

1. Contrast "the God whom the missionaries preached" and the images of Jesus they brought, with the discoveries Third World peoples made when they "began to read the Bible with new eyes." (30-36)

2. Why did people find Jesus' preaching about the Reign of God to be "subversive"? (37-39)

3. What is the basis for the insistent claim that "God is on the side of the poor, the oppressed, the persecuted"? (40-43) How is this related to the new view of Scripture and the person of Jesus Christ found therein?

4. Compare the understanding of *kairos* (43) in this document with that of the other *kairos* documents. How does this cumulative understanding prepare us to look for a *kairos* in the United States?

Chapter Three: Our Prophetic Mission

1. The chapter suggests that the basic sin is *idolatry*. Draw together other statements about idolatry in the other *kairos* documents as well. (46-61) How does the story of the Golden Calf symbolize this sin?

2. Examine the various characteristics of idolaters (50-61). In each case describe specific examples of idolatry in our own society. (This may take a long time. . . .) Are there idols present in our own nation of which the document seems unaware?

3. The rest of the chapter gives four specific examples of idolatry: heresy (62-71), apostasy (72-75), hypocrisy (76-79), and blasphemy (80-82). Examine each brand of idolatry in relation to such questions as the following:

    a. what is the distinctive emphasis?

    b. are the examples given clear and fair?

    c. where do we see examples of each brand of idolatry in our own national life?

    d. how can each brand be rooted out of our national life?

4. The statement that will provoke the most discussion will undoubtedly be: "We denounce all forms of right-wing Christianity as heretical." (63) What exactly are the signers of the document

referring to? What examples of the characteristics of right-wing Christianity listed in the document have you observed? If you do not feel indicted as a right-wing Christian by these paragraphs, what do you learn about shortcomings and perils in your own faith stance? What are the chief signs of idolatry, heresy, hypocrisy, and blasphemy in our nation as a whole?

Chapter Four: The Call to Conversion

1. The title and theme of the document are drawn from the "Damascus Road" experience of Saul of Tarsus. (83-85) Read the account of Saul's conversion in Acts 9:1-30. What parallels do you find between his experience and the experience the writers of the document commend to all of us? (86-91)

2. Compare the writers' acknowledgment that they, too, need conversion (91) with similar acknowledgments in the other two documents. What does this say about our own need for conversion?

Conclusion

1. In light of the devastating analysis of the state of the world and the state of the church, what basis for hope emerges?

2. How can we relate that hope to the reality of "pain, suffering and many deaths" that describe the future of committed Christians?

3. How can we respond creatively to the gracious plea of the writers that we, who live in "industrial capitalist countries," begin to "build a network of exchange and cooperation"?

Is It Time for a
Kairos USA Document?

A Preliminary Investigation

The writers of all three documents in this book believe they are living in a *kairos* situation, a time of judgment and opportunity, fraught with decisive consequences for good or evil, and that they must respond to it. There is no reason to doubt the correctness of their assessment.

A hard choice follows: Do we in the United States also live in a *kairos* situation? Or are we something of an exception, doing pretty well at a time when others are stumbling? Would it not be guilt-mongering, or at least gloom-mongering, to paint our situation as darkly as they paint theirs? We could surely improve things, but, equally surely, things are not as bad as our Third World friends suggest. Or are they?

A resolution of this dilemma depends, of course, on who is doing the resolving. Many, probably most, middle-class North Americans will be unconvinced by a negative analysis of our own situation, believing that with whatever problems we have, we are the brilliant (or lucky) exception to the ills of modernity. But if we ask women among that same middle-class, and particularly women of any class who are single parents trying to survive on welfare, whether things are well with them, we will assuredly get a different answer. If we

143

extend the group of respondents to members of the black community, we will find an even bleaker assessment of our society emerging, accompanied by much pain and considerable anger. The same would be true for other minority groups—Hispanics, Asian-Americans, gays, lesbians, the physically handicapped, and so on. Children, particularly children of minority races in single-parent families, would have the most heart-rending tales of all.

If we are sensitive to such responses, we have to conclude that things are not well in the body politic of the United States of America.

"Discerning the Signs of the Times"

Since one of the tasks of a *kairos* document is to "discern the signs of the times"—something the writers of the three documents do with devastating accuracy and honesty—we must see what kinds of "signs" are actually present in our own society. At a conference at Kirkridge, Pennsylvania, in the fall of 1989 dealing with *kairos* themes, participants identified the following characteristics of our own situation:

- We are a society given to consumptive addiction, feeling that more "things" will bring us more fulfillment. The shopping mall is our new place of worship.
- The global economy brings massive wealth to a few (like us), and imposes unbelievable poverty on the overwhelming majority (the rest of the human family). The story line of our times is clear: the rich get richer and the poor get poorer. There is a causal connection.
- In some parts of the church a "second Reformation" is occurring, a shift from "salvation by faith alone" to "good news to the poor." We are loathe to admit this. It threatens us.
- We believe that we have "won" the Cold War, because "communist" societies are falling apart, and we assume that this proves the superiority of capitalism, even though the arms race continues unabated, our government continues to support dictatorial regimes, and the economic and social crisis for the world's poor only gets worse.
- We resist acknowledging that the real struggle is no longer be-

tween East and West (translation: the USSR vs. the USA), but between North and South (translation: rich vs. poor, white-skinned vs. dark-skinned, oppressors vs. oppressed).

- The so-called "war on drugs" is used to justify our military presence in many parts of the world (most recently in Peru), in a script reminiscent of the Vietnam buildup, deflecting billions of dollars needed for meeting the most elemental human needs at home.
- We respond only after-the-fact to environmental crises (oil spills, toxic dumps, nuclear plant mishaps), failing to realize that there are *structural* causes for these disasters built into the way we organize our economic life.
- Ugly clashes between races are increasing rather than decreasing, in suburban environments as well as in crowded cities, at home as well as abroad.
- We are being urged to give uncritical allegiance to our country (symbolized in frenetic discussions about "flag-burning"), failing to see that the American dream is not so much a fast buck as "liberty and justice for all." To suggest that we are subverting that ideal is to be labeled unpatriotic.
- Religion is widely used as a cloak to legitimate all of the above activities and many more.

A similar gathering, this time of the Community of St. Martin in Minneapolis, Minnesota, identified the following symptoms of a deep religious and political crisis in our society:

1. *Structural injustice within the world economy is responsible for massive death and destruction of the world's poor.* More than 40 million people die each year from hunger or hunger-related causes. Christians living in the leading capitalist power have particular responsibility for the injustices within the international economy. The victimization of the poor linked to the world economy also has many faces at home: infant mortality, inadequate health care, homelessness.

2. *The United States is actively engaged in warfare against the poor.* In the aftermath of the Vietnam war we have revived our war-making capacity to intervene in the Third World through "low-intensity conflict," a strategy through which we

seek to maintain our privileged position within the unjust world economy. It is a strategy against the poor that embraces terrorism and subverts democracy.

3. *Present global patterns of production and consumption become a war against future generations* undermining the support base for all life. We are participating in a scandalous attack on God's created order. The poisoning of air and water, depletion of the ozone layer, and climatic changes through a "greenhouse effect" are warning signs of an impending environmental catastrophe.

4. *The arms race victimizes the poor* by diverting human and natural resources from development into warfare, aggravates the environmental crisis and threatens the destruction of God's creation. Even in the new, more "relaxed" situation, first strike weapons fundamentally escalate the dangers of the arms race.

The Need for Confession

Many other lists could be produced to indicate that something is deeply amiss at the roots of our national life. Will we listen? Most North Americans want to avoid such an analysis. When President Carter suggested a decade ago the need to examine our national "malaise," this counted against him in the polls. Apparently, we want to hear only good things about ourselves—one way to account for the immense popularity of Mr. Carter's successor, who told us continually not only that all was well, but that things were getting even better. Such naivete is already reaping ugly dividends as we enter a new decade.

Even if only a fraction of the crisis points identified above were accurate, there would be a paramount need for soul-searching. Christians define this corporate reflection as "confession," the need to acknowledge our own complicity in ruptures of the social good. From a Christian perspective, confession is an absolute prerequisite for change. What might it involve? We turn again to the Community of St. Martin:

> 1. We need to confess that, despite verbal commitments to the contrary, our actions indicate confusion about our ultimate

allegiances. Our lives have been so coopted by our culture that faithfulness to the God of community, compassion and justice becomes nearly impossible. Wealth, power, security, capitalism, nationalism and patriotism are at present lords of our lives. In short, *idolatry* is our religious problem within the kairos time. We must boldly declare that uncritical patriotism and nationalism are brazen sins against God.

> This confession can lead us to reassert in word and
> deed our fundamental affirmation: Christ, not Caesar,
> is Lord.

2. We need to confess that our subservience to idols within the culture (wealth, power, nationalism, etc.) results in our participation in policies and systems that tear apart the body of Christ.

> This confession can lead us to reassert our commit-
> ment to the unity of the body of Christ which tran-
> scends national boundaries and ideologies.

3. We need to confess that our relative affluence is directly connected to widespread indifference to the suffering of the poor and the lack of bold action on behalf of and with the poor. We conform to the values and institutions of our society as long as our security is grounded in them. The promise of benefits from the dominant society distorts our faith and our politics.

> This confession can lead us to affirm a just and com-
> passionate God whose ideal for the human community
> is shalom, and to develop sustainable lifestyles so that
> our security is grounded in community and faith.

4. We need to confess that our subservience to the gods of the dominant culture is a stumbling block to authentic hope. The "false gods" do not satisfy our spiritual hunger and lead to emptiness and despair. Hope depends on our ability to confront problems that the dominant society encourages us to ignore, and inappropriate coping mechanisms (such as drugs, consumerism or escapist religion) deepen our sense of alienation.

> This confession can lead us to affirm our faith in a
> God of hope and liberation, who overcomes sin, en-

ables conversion and offers a Kingdom partially embodied in alternative futures.

(Note: The above reports from Kirkridge and the Community of St. Martin
have been slightly condensed and edited for inclusion in this volume. Further
help in dealing with these issues can be found in Nelson-Pallmeyer, *The War
against the Poor,* Orbis Books, Maryknoll, 1988, especially Ch. 5, "Faith and
Empire".)

Query: Can There Be a Single *Kairos USA* Document?

The question must be faced by all who want a prophetic *kairos*
document to emerge in the United States. The problem is one of
multiple and possibly contradictory agendas. For while whites, blacks,
women, gays/lesbians, and other groups share many concerns, each
group also has unique concerns that could be lost under too wide an
umbrella.

So there is something to be said for urging each group to go its
own way, articulate it own special concerns with utter clarity (and
anger, if need be), pull no punches, and challenge the rest of the
church in the most forthright manner possible, toning down nothing
for the sake of an overall consensus.

On the other hand, there are reasons for trying to create a single
document. The most basic of these is a realization that the "principalities and powers" would like nothing better than to have their
challengers fighting each other so energetically that they have no
strength left to attack a common enemy. "Divide and rule" is a
universal formula for staying in power.

Another reason for trying to produce a single document is that
whether the attempt succeeds or not, all those involved in the process
will be further sensitized and "conscienticized" by the need to confront perspectives to which they had not been exposed so directly.
The net result of this exercise, whatever the outcome, will be the
creation of better informed constituencies, and the possibility, at least,
of a wider "united front."

A Checklist of Concerns

What kind of concerns would a *Kairos USA* document contain? It would be presumptuous for any individual to attempt to dictate the agenda for others, but since the only way to begin a process is to begin, here is an initial proposal of items that might be included. The list is not complete, and readers are invited to use it merely as a "thought-starter," and to delete and augment at will.

___ an acknowledgment of the essential correctness of the overall analysis contained in the earlier *kairos* documents

___ a listing of our own "signs of the times" that make it a *kairos* for us

___ a confession of our complicity in the support and perpetuation of national and international structures of injustice

___ an acknowledgment of the failure of the church to speak prophetically to the needs of our time, and a plea to avoid timidity in the future

___ a willingness to learn from the insights of social analysis in combatting evil, coupled with a fresh look at the discrepancies between Christianity and capitalism

___ an analysis of the role of power in human society, with particular attention to our own abuse of it

___ a close look not only at international issues raised by the other *kairos* documents, but at our own *domestic* scene and the proliferation of such evils as racism, sexism, economic exploitation, denial of political and civil rights to minority groups, homelessness, over-inflated defense budgets, and so forth

___ treatment of specific sins in our society such as the new emphasis of our administration on "low-intensity conflict"

___ raising issues not directly discussed in the other documents, such as ecological concerns, the shedding of power, etc.

___ exploration of ways in which middle-class people can be transformed into agents of liberation

___ the use of biblical themes and images (idolatry, "serving in Pharaoh's court," temptation, repentance, death and resurrection) to clarify perspectives and provide new direction

___ fresh commitment to the "dangerous memory of Jesus," his teaching and example, as a basis for liberation

___ commitment to costly proposals by the signatories (changes of lifestyle, tax resistance, commitment to civil disobedience, etc.)

___ a clear message of hope as the unique Christian contribution and resource for energy, involvement and risk-taking.

___

___

___   (others to be filled in by readers)

___

Nuts and Bolts: A Modest Plan of Action

Whatever *Kairos USA* document or documents emerge will have only as much authority as their substantive messages can generate, for in the nature of the case there will be no "official" document by a denomination or ecumenical body. The process of creating *Kairos USA* will not come from on high, but will be generated out of the grassroots, as "ordinary" people here and there share their concerns and see them beginning to focus in overlapping ways. Many groups are already not only engaging in discussion but trying their hand at preliminary drafts of a *Kairos USA* document for our time.

One of the purposes of the present book, in addition to providing materials for such discussion, is to be a catalyst for the creation and extension of "Kairos Communities" that could form a network with much potential power. To that end, interested persons and groups are invited to communicate with an informal clearing house called

> The Committee of Correspondence
> 2021 28th Avenue South
> Minneapolis, Minnesota 55406

which will facilitate an exchange of information, ideas, names, groups, rough drafts, and so forth, so that interested groups can begin to link together.

An appropriate symbolic time for the release of a *Kairos USA* document would be October 12, 1992, the 500th anniversary of the so-called "discovery" of the new world by Columbus—the significance of which needs to be radically rethought, so that the evils perpetrated in those first five hundred years can be exposed, challenged and replaced by more worthy goals and structures in the second half of the millennium.

No one knows where a movement generated by the original *kairos* documents may go. If it is finally nothing more than our own human design, it will fail; but if it correctly reads the "signs of the times" as a time of *kairos* for all of us, in which God is seeking our involvement, there is nothing that will be able to stop it.

For Further Reading: A Sampling

Overall

"What Is Contextual Theology?" (Institute for Contextual Theology, P.O. Box 32047, Braamfontein 2017, South Africa). A brief presentation of the methodology of the *kairos* documents.

Ulrich Duchrow, *Global Economy: A Confessional Issue for the Churches?* World Council of Churches, Geneva, 1987. A challenging book on the need for a new economic structure.

Jack Nelson-Pallmeyer, *The War against the Poor,* Orbis, Maryknoll, 1988. An examination of the effects of "low-intensity conflict," the new instrument of U.S. foreign policy against the Third World.

Richard Shaull, *Naming the Idols,* Meyer-Stone, Oak Park, 1988. A treatment of the theme that pervades all the *kairos* documents, the power of idolatry.

Paul Tillich, chapter on "Kairos" in *The Protestant Era,* University of Chicago Press, Chicago, 1938; see also *Systematic Theology,* Vol. III. Theological treatments of the theme of *kairos.*

Robert McAfee Brown, *Gustavo Gutiérrez: An Introduction to Liberation Theology,* Orbis, Maryknoll, 1990. Chapter 7 relates the *kairos* documents to the overall liberation struggle abroad and at home.

South Africa

Willis Logan, ed., *The Kairos Covenant: Standing with South African Christians,* Friendship Press/Meyer-Stone, New York and Oak Park, 1988. Contains the full text of *The Kairos Document* together with essays on the three South African theologies.

Allan Boesak, *Comfort and Protest,* Westminster, Philadelphia, 1987. An example of the power of the biblical message in a situation of injustice.

Frank Chicane, *No Life of My Own,* Orbis, Maryknoll, 1989. The story of one of the persons involved in the creation of *The Kairos Document.*

John de Gruchy, *The Church Struggle in South Africa,* Eerdmans, Grand Rapids, 1979. Historical background for understanding recent events.

John de Gruchy and Charles Villa-Vicencio, eds., *Apartheid Is a Heresy,* Eerdmans, Grand Rapids, 1983. Documents that trace the development of a *status confessionis* in South Africa.

Albert Nolan, *God in South Africa,* Eerdmans, Grand Rapids, 1988. A statement of Christianity as seen from "the underside of history."

Charles Villa-Vicencio, *Trapped in Apartheid,* Orbis, Maryknoll, 1988. An indictment of the white "English-speaking" churches in South Africa that serves as a mirror for the sins of white English-speaking churches in North America.

Central America

Philip Berryman, *The Religious Roots of Rebellion: Christians in Central American Revolutions,* Orbis, Maryknoll, 1984. An extensive treatment of the church in Nicaragua, El Salvador and Guatemala.

Raymond Bonner, *Weakness and Deceit,* Times Books, New York, 1984. The story of U.S. intervention in the affairs of El Salvador.

Roy Gutman, *Banana Diplomacy,* Simon and Schuster, New York, 1988. The story of U.S. intervention in the affairs of Nicaragua.

Alfred T. Hennelly, ed., *Liberation Theology: A Documentary History,*

Orbis, Maryknoll, 1990. A collection of the primary sources for understanding liberation theology.

Walter LaFeber, *Inevitable Revolutions,* expanded edition, Norton, New York, 1988. A clear tracing of the last hundred years of U.S. intervention in the affairs of Central American countries.

Asia

Raymond Bonner, *Waltzing with a Dictator,* Vintage Books, New York, 1988. The story of the United States' attempts to support and legitimate the Marcos dictatorship.

Feliciano Cariño et al., *Theology, Politics and Struggle,* National Council of Churches, Manila, 1986. A collection of essays on struggles for creative revolution in the Philippines.

Commission on Theological Concerns, *Minjung Theology: People as the Subjects of History,* Orbis, Maryknoll, 1983. Essays on a peoples' theology that has emerged in Korea.

Virginia Fabella, ed., *Asia's Struggle for Full Humanity,* Orbis, Maryknoll, 1980. Papers from a conference in which Asians discussed problems and possibilities in their corporate struggle for liberation.

Thomas Marti et al., *Letter from the Philippines,* Philippine National Forum, Davao City, 1986 (available from Church Coalition for Human Rights in the Philippines, 110 Maryland Avenue, NW, Washington, D.C. 20002). A letter from U.S. missionaries in the Philippines, pleading for a revision of U.S. policy.

Aloysius Pieris, *An Asian Theology of Liberation,* Orbis, Maryknoll, 1988. Reflections of a Jesuit in Sri Lanka.

APPENDIX B

Groups Working on *Kairos* Issues

Committee of Correspondence
2021 28th Avenue South
Minneapolis, Minnesota 55406

Center of Concern
3700 13th Street N.E.
Washington, D.C. 20017

Institute for Contextual Theology
P.O. Box 32047
Braamfontein 2017, South Africa

Community of St. Martin
1929 South Fifth Street
Minneapolis, Minnesota 55454

New York Circus, Inc.
P.O. Box 37
Times Square Station
New York, NY 10108

Theology in a Global Context
475 Riverside Drive
New York, NY 11015

World Peacemakers, Inc.
2025 Massachusetts Avenue N.W.
Washington, D.C. 20036

Sojourners
P.O. Box 29272
Washington, D.C. 20017

Christianity and Crisis
537 W. 121st Street
New York, NY 10027

National Catholic Reporter
P.O. Box 281
Kansas City, Missouri 64141

Evangelicals for Social Action
10 Lancaster Ave.
Philadelphia, PA 19151

The Barmen Declaration

In view of the errors of the "German Christians" and of the present Reich Church Administration, which are ravaging the Church and at the same time also shattering the unity of the German Evangelical Church, we confess the following evangelical truths:

1. "I am the Way and the Truth and the Life; no one comes to the Father except through me." (Jn. 14:6)

"Truly, truly I say to you, he who does not enter the sheepfold through the door but climbs in somewhere else, he is a thief and a robber. I am the Door; if anyone enters through me, he will be saved." (Jn. 10:1, 9)

Jesus Christ, as he is attested to us in Holy Scripture, is the one Word of God which we have to hear, and which we have to trust and obey in life and in death.

We reject the false doctrine that the Church could and should recognize as a source of its proclamation, beyond and besides this one Word of God, yet other events, powers, historic figures, and truths as God's revelation.

2. "Jesus Christ has been made wisdom and righteousness and sanctification and redemption for us by God." (I Cor. 1:30)

As Jesus Christ is God's comforting pronouncement of the forgiveness of all our sins, so, and with equal seriousness, he is

also God's vigorous announcement of his claim upon our whole life. Through him there comes to us joyful liberation from the godless ties of this world for free, grateful service to his creatures.

We reject the false doctrine that there could be areas of our life in which we would belong not to Jesus Christ but to other lords, areas in which we would not need justification and sanctification through him.

3. "Let us, however, speak the truth in love, and in every respect grow into him who is the head, into Christ, from whom the whole body is joined together." (Eph. 4:15-16)

The Christian Church is the community of brethren in which, in Word and sacrament, through the Holy Spirit, Jesus Christ acts in the present as Lord. With both its faith and its obedience, with both its message and its order, it has to testify in the midst of the sinful world, as the Church of pardoned sinners, that it belongs to him alone and lives and may live by his comfort and under his direction alone, in expectation of his appearing.

We reject the false doctrine that the Church could have permission to hand over the form of its message and of its order to whatever it itself might wish or to the vicissitudes of the prevailing ideological and political convictions of the day.

4. "You know that the rulers of the Gentiles exercise authority over them and those in high position lord it over them. So shall it not be among you; but if anyone would have authority over you, let him be your servant." (Matt. 20:25-26)

The various offices in the Church do not provide a basis for some to exercise authority over others but for the ministry with which the whole community has been entrusted and charged to be carried out.

We reject the false doctrine that, apart from this ministry, the Church could, and could have permission to, give itself or allow itself to be given special leaders *(Führer)* vested with ruling authority.

5. "Fear God, honour the King?" (I Pet. 2:17)

Scripture tells us that by divine appointment the State, in this still unredeemed world in which also the Church is situated, has

the task of maintaining justice and peace, so far as human discernment and human ability make this possible, by means of the threat and use of force. The Church acknowledges with gratitude and reverence toward God the benefit of this, his appointment. It draws attention to God's Kingdom (Reich), God's commandment and justice, and with these the responsibility of those who rule and those who are ruled. It trusts and obeys the power of the Word, by which God upholds all things.

We reject the false doctrine that beyond its special commission the State should and could become the sole and total order of human life and so fulfil the vocation of the Church as well.

We reject the false doctrine that beyond its special commission the Church should and could take on the nature, tasks and dignity which belong to the State and thus become itself an organ of the State.

6. "See, I am with you always, to the end of the age." (Matt. 28:20) "God's Word is not fettered." (II Tim. 2:9)

The Church's commission, which is the foundation of its freedom, consists in this: in Christ's stead, and so in the service of his own Word and work, to deliver to all people, through preaching and sacrament, the message of the free grace of God.

We reject the false doctrine that with human vainglory the Church could place the Word and work of the Lord in the service of self-chosen desires, purposes and plans.

The Confessional Synod of the German Evangelical Church declares that it sees in the acknowledgement of these truths and in the rejection of these errors the indispensable theological basis of the German Evangelical Church as a confederation of Confessional Churches. It calls upon all who can stand in solidarity with its Declaration to be mindful of these theological findings in all their decisions concerning Church and State. It appeals to all concerned to return to unity in faith, hope and love.

Verbum Dei manet in aeternum.

DATE DUE

~~AUG 1 8 1998~~			
GAYLORD			PRINTED IN U.S.A.